Praise for *Goat Lips* ...

"Matthew Taylor's tales resemble the English ale that got him into such a memorable fix in *Goat Lips*. The ⸢ light and refreshing, a second is decidedly r⸢ d each successive draught bring⸢ ʼo the bittersweet caverns ⸢ ʼr news: you'll wake up v ⸢fully reaching for anot⸢

⸝aniel Glick, Author,
⸝y *Dancing: A Father, Two Kids,
and a Jou. ⸝y to the Ends of the Earth* (PublicAffairs)

"Matthew Taylor's short essays are much more than mere entertainment. They are each a guide on how to deftly (and humorously) maneuver life's persistent questions and quandaries, all the while instructing you to—above all—smile, relax and enjoy every moment."

~ Mollie O'Brien, Grammy Award-Winning
Singer/Recording Artist

"Reading Matthew Taylor's *Goat Lips—Tales of a Lapsed Englishman,* your journey through his (mis)adventures and responses to each drives home the message that indeed, 'Life Is Good.'"

~ Rich Moore
Guitarist/Recording Artist

"These are the words and stories that we all want to tell but never do. This compilation of close-to-the-heart stories rings true—too, they are simply hilarious and heart rendering (yes, some tales bring tears of true joy and others, tears of recognition as we see the warmth of family and humanity shine). Matthew Taylor, the lips of the goat who lives in Goat Lips Cottage, is a born geographer—his words leave us with a strong sense of place, both here and 'there.' Hold on tight for some fast-paced reading. We want more like this, Matthew."

~ Matthew J. Taylor (Not me!)
Professor of Geography, University of Denver

"Absolutely Bloody Brilliant."

~ Matthew J. Taylor
(Okay this is me! Ignore this one.)

"At one point in this sublimely amusing collection of stories, Anglo-American author Mathew Taylor accuses himself of possessing a 'cynical nature,' to which his readers will surely cry as one: Au contraire, Pierre! Mr. Taylor's writing is sweet and wise and laugh-out-loud funny, but never, ever snarky or snide. And that refreshing lack of ironic detachment is just one of the book's myriad pleasures. Each story is a perfect little gem unto itself, but taken together, they create a marvelous picture of a wonderful life being thumpingly well-lived."

~ Anthony Powell
Artistic Director, Stories on Stage

"The combination of evocative prose; a strong, likable, and honest narrator's voice; and an ability to find humor (and wisdom) in challenging moments, makes Goat Lips a winner."

~ Mark Tuchman
Creative Director, School Library Journal

"Matthew Taylor is a natural born storyteller. The stories in this collection are told with self-deprecating wit, charm and honesty. And, of course, he's got those lips too."

Steven Cole Hughes,
Award-Winning Playwright, *Billy Hell*

GOAT LIPS

GOAT LIPS

Tales of a Lapsed Englishman

Matthew Taylor

MERRY DISSONANCE PRESS   CASTLE ROCK, CO

Goat Lips:
Tales of a Lapsed Englishman

Published by Merry Dissonance Press, LLC
Castle Rock, CO

FIRST EDITION 2015

Library of Congress Control Number: 2014917587
Taylor, Matthew, Author
Goat Lips: Tales of a Lapsed Englishman
Matthew Taylor

ISBN 978-1-939919-02-1
1. Biography & Autobiography
2. Humor

Book Design and Cover Design © 2015
Cover Photo by Paul Orosz
Cover Design by Victoria Wolf
Bio Photo by Brian Kozak
Illustrations by Catherine McNeil
Book Design by Andrea Costantine
Editing by Bobby Haas and Donna Mazzitelli

All Rights Reserved by Matthew Taylor
and Merry Dissonance Press, LLC

With respect, some names have been changed.

In memory of
Sylvia E. Taylor,
my loving mother
and
Art Thilquist,
my dear friend
May you both rest peacefully with the
angels

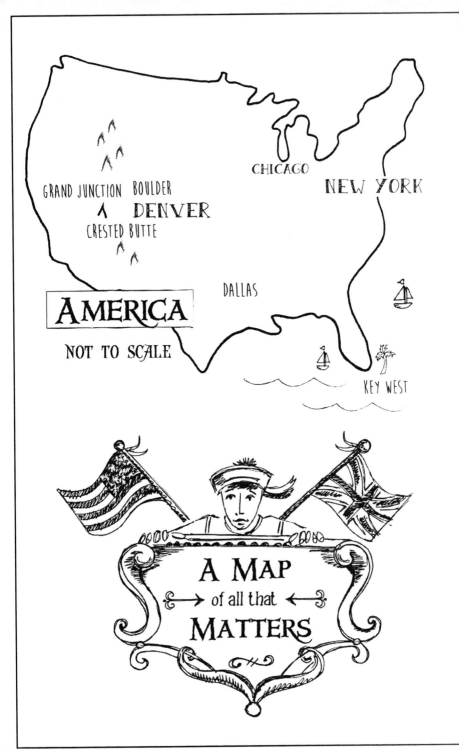

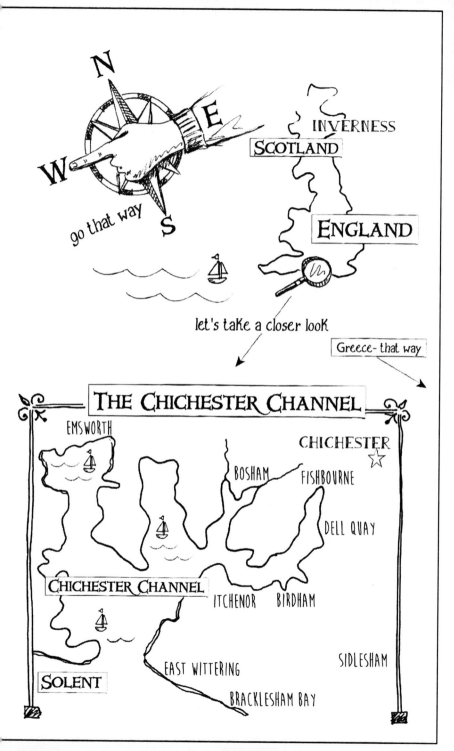

Contents

*"My life would have made a better book
if things had happened in this order." ~MT*

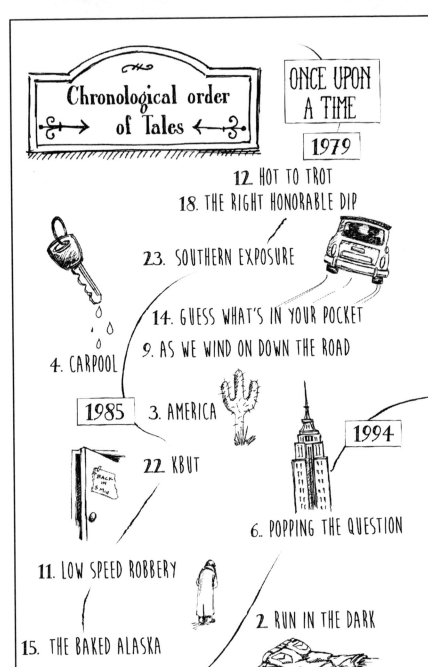

FOREWORD

I KNEW MATTHEW and I were going to be close friends the first time I hoisted him up onto my back, half-naked and covered in baby powder. I was right. And it was the first of hundreds of times we performed our ridiculous parody of a Cirque du Soleil-style balancing act that became a staple of our comedy trio, A.C.E. (American, Canadian, Englishman). I am the American, Matthew the Englishman, and our long-time creative partner, Barbara Gehring, represented the Great White North.

In the midst of creating over fifty original A.C.E. comedy shows and traveling extensively to add our unique brand of humor to countless events all over North America and Europe, Matthew and I created a close bond that is more similar to siblings than friends. This level of intimacy proved essential when we embarked on the journey we referred to only as "The Book."

I felt Matthew Taylor's wit and insight needed to be shared with a larger audience than the hearty clumps of fans who doggedly showed up for his monthly live storytelling events in Denver. Although his experience as a self-described "Englishman trapped in an American's body" might be unique, his stories are very accessible to all. Actually, their allure is so great that my husband Paul and I flew Matthew out to England to greet us as we disembarked from our honeymoon crossing aboard the QE2 from New York to Southampton, just so he could tour us around for a couple of days, telling his stories in the places where they actually happened. I remember looking out the window of the Anchor Bleu and across the inlet, imagining Matthew's 1979 red Vauxhall Cavalier slowly being swallowed by the Chichester Channel and then traveling the winding way to a stubble-filled cornfield near Sidlesham, seeing the police close on our tail with sirens blaring.

A few years later when our beloved Canadian's attention turned for a time to birthing her beautiful little girl, Isabella, I suggested to Matthew that this lull might be a good time for him to push out his own little bundle … of stories.

Matthew is a story conduit. Life goes through him and comes out stories. Stories gush out of him uncontrollably. I am pretty sure he even thinks in story form. Some people are fluent in a foreign language. Matthew is fluent in story.

I would like to say that I made the suggestion to Matthew to start writing and immediately he began typing up the crazy tales I'd heard told over many beers to many ears for many years. But alas, I had to poke, prod, and pester before he ever put pencil to paper. (Actually, I even had to buy the pencil and paper for him.) Once he found it wasn't as difficult as he had imagined the stack of yellow legal tablets full of his impossibly small handwriting got taller and taller.

I left him to his scribblings for a while, when Barbara came out of the baby vortex long enough for her and me to polish up our comedy show, *Girls Only – The Secret Comedy of Women,* and parade it around in front of some producers. To our delight, the show was immediately swept up in a theatrical pixie dust storm and ended up on stage at the Denver Center for the Performing Arts for two years before it moved on to more productions across North America. During this time of distraction, I relished the quieter, less bombastic project of Matthew's book. While the *Girls Only* storm raged outside, we would sit at his dining room table for hours, quietly punching up his writing, searching for the perfect synonyms, and discussing the more esoteric aspects of comedy. "Is *second cousin* funnier than *cousin*?"

Long before the book was ready for publishing, we felt the need to give the project a little PR boost and get Matthew back into the public eye to create anticipation. Our answer to this was a reading and book signing event. Matthew read several of his written stories to a packed house and then afterward signed books. Not his own books, mind you, as his had not been published yet. His fans loved the devilment of it and brought a wide variety of books for Matthew to sign, from Sarah Palin's autobiography to a children's bible. It was innocent mischief like this that has always been the backbone of our comedic impulses, and it reinvigorated us.

Over the years everyone saw me by Matthew's side, as we plugged away at the book, but we never had a good answer for what my role was in this project. I'm not the author, and I'm definitely not an editor either. Maybe I am the book's midwife. The skillset is similar to a baby midwife. It takes a cool head, stamina, and a gentle touch.

This book was definitely born breach. The stories were told first and then written, which makes for a trickier delivery. After a spate of fevered activity, the project would hit a lull, contractions would cease, and Matthew would have to walk around with the book sticking halfway out of him for months at a time. It was very uncomfortable. Eventually, the discomfort would bring him back to the project at hand. I was always ready with ice chips (usually floating in bourbon poured by my husband) and encouragement. "Push, Matthew, push!" Sometimes the view wasn't pretty, but bringing this book into the world has been one of the most satisfying creative projects of my career.

After all of these years, spending time with Matthew still fills me with expectant giddiness, like we're hiding behind a couch ready to jump out for a surprise party, barely able to contain our exuberance. His ability to question the assumptions of everyday life with a wry grin and a twinkle in his kind eyes makes Matthew endlessly entertaining. His lighthearted spirit illuminates everything around him with a joyful glow. I am fortunate to have spent so much time in such close proximity to so much genius ... and I have the baby powder in my ears to prove it.

~ Linda Klein
Co-Founder, A.C.E. Entertainment

1
GOAT LIPS PART I

IN THE MIDST OF A BUSY, hot, Colorado summer day, the phone rang. It was my talent agent, Patty Kingsbaker. "Matthew, can you make an audition for a television commercial this afternoon at three o'clock?" I was already juggling several balls, and throwing an audition into the mix would be impossible. So, I replied, "Yes, of course."

Patty explained, "This audition is right up your alley. It's all facial expressions and only three words." I had to agree, it definitely played to my strengths.

Later that day, hot and flustered, at two minutes to three, I tore into the parking lot of Colorado Casting.

With headshot in hand I dashed into the reception area, signed in, grabbed a copy of the storyboard, said hi to all the usual suspects awaiting their turn, and plunked myself down in an available chair. I took a deep breath. I calmed myself and started to prepare.

The storyboard (a series of rough cartoon drawings depicting the shots and general idea of the commercial) was, at first glance, somewhat unclear to me. Only upon closer inspection did I realize something remarkable; I was in a room with twelve other gentlemen all waiting patiently for a turn to audition to be the lips of a goat.

Having seen the sign-in sheet, I was aware that thirty pairs of lips had preceded us and another twenty to thirty pairs were sure to follow. That is somewhere in the region of seventy sets of lips auditioning in an attempt to find the most goat-like lips possible. Any way you look at it, that's a pretty hefty lip search.

Slightly puzzled, I thought I might as well make the most of it and give it my best shot. Having never owned a goat, I realized I wasn't sure what goat lips looked like. The more I attempted to conjure up the face of a goat in my mind, the blanker the general lip vicinity tended to be. Eventually I had to question whether goats actually have lips at all.

I even glanced around for hidden cameras, thinking that this could be a perfect candid camera moment. I imagined myself standing in front of a camera, thoughtfully manipulating my lips so as to best emulate a goat while millions of Americans watched—all laughing and saying to each other, "Look at that fool. Doesn't he know goats don't have lips?"

Once I delved deeper into the storyboard, my fears that this was a ruse lessened. I noted the client was Miller Light. Beer commercials usually mean anything can happen and there need be no rhyme or reason. With the reassurance that I was auditioning not only for a "real" job but also for a "National Commercial," I decided to model my lips after a generic goat, because as I tried to picture a famous goat to imitate, I realized, rather sadly, that there simply weren't any.

As I prepared I could sense my confidence growing. *I am going to be the best lips of a goat they will ever see.*

They called my name. It was "show time."

I strutted into the room, filled with the confidence of a man at the top of his game. Peggy from Colorado Casting introduced me to the clients, all seven of them, seated behind two folding tables. A video camera on a tripod stood in front of them. I gave everybody a cheery "Hi" and handed Peggy my headshot. One of the seven looked up wearily and said, "Hello." What he really meant to say was, "We will probably never see you or your lips again."

Peggy directed me to a small black X on the floor, about ten feet in front of the table, and asked me to slate for the camera. To oblige I looked deep into the lens, summoned my inner goat, and said, "Hi, I'm Matthew Taylor with Donna Baldwin Talent." I realized this would be the only moment for my facial features to be seen as a collection.

Peggy turned the camera off and gave me some quick instructions. "I'm going to be in a close-up on your lips, so be a goat. Then, after about twenty seconds say, 'Life is Good' as a goat." *Simple enough instructions,* I thought. Yet I wondered, *What does "be a goat" and "as a goat" really mean?* As I pondered this, the camera approached within a foot of my nose, and before I had time to think further, the red light popped on.

I started to do what I considered to be "goat-like" movements with my lips. Unfortunately, the reflection in the camera lens acted as a mirror, forcing me to watch every earnest movement of my aspiring goat lips—which (if I'm being completely truthful) was just me randomly moving my lips around.

After what seemed like an eternity of inventive lip movement, it was time to deliver the big line. I said, "Life is good." The red light promptly went off. I heard an abrupt "thank you" and was shown the door. Peggy walked me out, and as I exited she whispered, "You were great." I always liked Peggy.

So, that was that. On the drive home, I kept my eyes peeled just in case there was a goat strolling through Denver. I was anxious to compare our lips.

At 7:00 p.m. that same night, my agent called.

"Matthew, good job. They've got you on hold."

I asked, "How does that work?"

She explained, "You are the best goat lips currently available in Denver, but they're off to audition in LA and New York over the next two days."

My heart sank. The goat lips in LA were sure to be beautiful. And as for the New York goat lips, well, they would all be classically trained. The competition would be intense, the pressure for two days unbearable. I opted for the simple route—I pretended to forget all about it.

So, you can imagine my surprise when the phone rang two days later and Patty said, "You're hired. Your shoot is at LSI studios on Tuesday at 6:00 a.m."

I put the phone down. Pride welled up inside me. My chest inflated, my cheeks flushed, my jaw set, and my gaze fixed into the middle distance.

I ... me ...

Matthew Taylor ...

have the best goat lips ...

in America!

2
Run in the Dark

THE WORST THING about breaking up with someone is that you're forced to start dating again. Before I got married, I was a "five-year-relationship" kind of guy. I had enjoyed two five-year relationships, one in England and one in America. So that meant I'd had ten glorious years of not having to get a date.

Dating does not come easily to me. I'm not able to stroll up to a strange woman and start or, more importantly, sustain casual conversation. I also have to admit the sad but true fact that I have never even asked a lady to dance. It's not that I dislike dancing. It's just that anywhere dancing is an option, there is also a bar. Admittedly, I am more comfortable asking a bartender for a drink than a girl for a dance.

Some say drinking is a great step forward in the pursuit of meeting women. The more you drink, the more your loins start to tingle. Your urge for a woman's company increases. But sadly for me, I was dealt a couple of genetic blows. When I drink, I just become thirstier. The more I drink, the greater the thirst grows. The worst thing is I never really get that drunk. So I just happily sit there and drink and drink and drink. Unfortunately, I'm also not good-looking enough to have girls approach me very often. Usually, it's about once every five years. When, on the rare occasion a woman does pursue me, I work very hard to make the most of it. Foremost in my mind? *This could mean five more years of not dating.*

One such rare night presented itself soon after I'd broken up with my five-year American relationship. Even though I had been jettisoned not only from the relationship, but also from her apartment, I had become smitten enough with Boulder, Colorado to stick around and find alternative accommodations. Back in the dating game, on many evenings I found myself in one of Boulder's half-dozen night clubs. Since I was a single man once more, I'd made a solemn vow to play the game. *Approach women, make casual conversation. Do the leg work — laugh, dance, be merry. This time things will be different. Watch out women! Matthew's single again and he means business!*

It was no surprise to me that on this particular night I found myself at the bar at 12:45 a.m. accompanied by a raging thirst … and nothing else. I guess talk is cheap. Unless that talk is, *I'll have another gin and tonic,* in which case it is about eight dollars.

I sat in the sweltering night club, busily wearing a hole in my bar stool, contemplating my general parchedness. I gazed through the layers of smoke towards the garishly lit familiar liquor bottles that danced seductively in front of me. On the verge of succumbing to their wily charms, I was rescued by an attractive young lady who plonked herself down next to me and started to chat away as if we had known each other for years.

This wasn't the usual "bar chat." There was substance within the conversation, or at least as much substance as can be yelled over the furious bass line being hammered out from the speakers twelve feet from my ears. I offered her a drink, but she refused, saying she really didn't like to drink too much. She had a spirited gleam in her eyes as she spoke, and her long dark hair bounced playfully every time she cocked her head to one side, listening intently to my every word. Here was a woman who was adventurous, fun, smart, and different. *Could it be that I was meeting my Ms. Right? (At least five years' worth?)*

We danced the rest of the night together—laughing, smiling, and spinning our way into the wee hours of the morning. There were rough attempts at introductions shouted through the dense music towards various friends of hers, but I paid little attention. To me, we were the only two in the whole club.

Suddenly, it was over. Mid-song, the music crashed into silence. Harsh, bright, florescent lights popped on everywhere, forcing me to focus on my previously unseen surroundings. Quickly, I came to the uncomfortable realization that earlier in the evening, when fully sober, I had made a conscious decision to spend my entire evening in a dirty, run-down dump.

I watched the few remaining people huddle together, trying desperately to come up with a plan for after-hours revelry. They were all committed to avoiding that total party failure—going home to sleep—since sleeping is really only for those who want to feel great in the morning.

After some group yelling, during which I was sorely tempted to explain that the music had stopped and we could resume talking at a normal level, my dream lady shouted at me, "Hey, a group of us are going swimming in the Boulder Reservoir. Wanna come along?" My first reaction was, *Damn, why didn't I bring my swimming things?* Luckily, I was still in control enough to keep that thought to myself. My verbal response was much better, "That would be great! Let's go."

We bundled out of the Club de la Dumpo, and six of us squeezed into a small car. We sped off into the dark. Destination: Boulder Reservoir. With a disembodied elbow firmly wedged between my third and fourth rib, I pondered the merit of being crammed into a Dodge Dart full of strangers, one of whom was a woman I madly wanted to impress, all headed towards a reservoir in the wee hours of the morning with the certainty that upon arrival I would be expected to remove all articles of clothing and throw myself into the icy cold blackness. However thirsty I had become during the night and however hard I'd worked to cure that thirst, it obviously wasn't hard enough for a time such as this.

It appeared I wasn't the only one contemplating the current situation. Generally speaking, everybody had been eager to feign overwhelming support for the naked proposal, but once the plan was put into action, the majority of participants began to ask themselves critical questions such as, "Why?" Our internal questioning manifested itself in the form of a cold, dark silence that prevailed as we sped towards the reservoir.

When we arrived, we all happily toppled out of our cramped, tension-filled quarters and surveyed our surroundings. I heard people whisper, "Wow, it's so beautiful!" and "What a perfect night."

The sight I beheld was indeed stunning. Boulder Reservoir lay in front of us, still and silent, its watery fingers stretching out in different directions. Between each finger was a small sandy beach. The light sand created a stark contrast to the water. The surface of the lake was perfectly smooth, upon which danced the reflection of a full moon. A path of shimmering light skated across the water towards us, as if it were nature's way of inviting us in.

The scene was breathtaking. It was truly "a perfect night." Sounding the battle cry, our fearsome band of warriors broke the night's peaceful perfection and set off at full-tilt, sprinting down to the sandy beach.

Nakedness is a strange thing. It's cool to be casual about it, but in all honesty, the thousands of years it's been deemed important to cover our bodies have taken their toll. Our natural state has become a very unnatural condition. Few people seem to be at ease with their nakedness. Or, for that matter, even the proposition of being naked. We were no different.

Having arrived at the water's edge with great gusto, it was remarkable how quickly our gusto evaporated. We hovered around awkwardly. We knew what was expected, but each of us stood unwilling to be the first to strip and then dip.

I'd been confronted with skinny-dipping before and from that experience devised myself a foolproof plan for success. (By the way, any time someone feels compelled to use the word "foolproof," a good rule of thumb is to insert the word "not" before it.) My foolproof plan was simple: Be first.

This philosophy works on several levels. However uncomfortable it may feel, by simply stripping down and charging in first, you appear to be a brave, wild, risk-taking, first-in kind of guy with whom everybody wants to associate. Far more important, you are in front of everybody. Meaning everybody is viewing this brave, wild, risk-taking, first-in kind of guy from the rear. This affords what I best describe as a "plain buttock view." The obvious benefit is that buttocks are buttocks, similar for both men and women, so there is simply less interest. It is rare to hear people marvel at one another's buttocks.

Another valuable point in being first—you are quickly below the waterline, and basically fully clothed again, albeit in a chilly, watery gown. You can yell encouragement to the others from the safety of your harbor and even engage in a little viewing, if you are of that ilk. First-in is definitely the way to go.

With this in mind, I gave a glance towards my fellow skinny-dippers and to my horror, realized they too had foolproof plans. After the brief pause at the waterline, everybody had overcome their awkwardness and decided the "me first" principle was in order. Most people already had a considerable head start on me in the clothes removal department.

As I raced to catch up, I could not help but notice that the woman of my dreams was right next to me effortlessly removing clothing at high speed, while I struggled to yank, tug, and rip at every article in my attempt to shed clothing from my body. *I have to be first!* I was sure my relationship depended on it.

Suddenly, we were both naked and heading for the water in a dead heat, stride for stride. Down the gently sloping sand we galloped. Picking up speed, we hit the shallows with enough momentum to carry us into the deep water within seconds. Still neck and neck, we raced through the shallow water. It was only a matter of time before the deep water would engulf us both. <u>*But how much time?*</u>

We'd been running for ten seconds, which, it turns out, is a very long time when you're naked. And we were still in only about eight inches of water. I increased my pace, but twenty-five seconds into the sprint and a good thirty yards from the shore, we were still only shin deep. It was at this point that a sick and desperate feeling swept over me. I had worked it out. I continued to run but knew to my horror that we were running on an inconveniently placed sand bar.

The word "clothing" dates back to the early-something times. It's a good word. But I would like to take this opportunity to change the word "clothing" and improve upon it. My suggestion is "jiggle stoppers." Because that is what clothing does. It stops the jiggle. When the human body is left au naturel it takes an incredibly minimal amount of movement to generate a jiggle. Where the jiggle occurs varies considerably.

Male jiggle areas are different from female jiggle areas. Large people may jiggle in different places than small people, old people in different places than young people. But the constant remains. We all jiggle. All the time, if left unrestricted. It is therefore only natural for us to don jiggle stoppers, so the world can continue to function as we know it and not spin uncontrollably into one mad jiggle-fest.

As I entered into my forty-sixth second of running across a sandbar, naked with total strangers, two things became very clear to me. First, the old sentimental ballad "By the Light of the Silvery Moon" bore absolutely no relationship to this evening. The full moon hanging majestically in the perfectly clear sky was acting more like a large, unforgiving halogen lamp. Sadly, visibility was not a problem.

Second, jiggling. At first I became acutely aware of my own jiggle. And as I looked around to see if anybody noticed, it was impossible not to notice other people's jiggles. Of course, noticing their jiggles meant they were surely noticing mine. With no end in immediate sight, still running at full speed, I attempted to use my hand as a jiggle stopper. It slowed me down, but some form of restriction was oddly comforting. I glanced at my companion and she too had resorted to a similar tactic in an effort to conceal her jiggling areas.

We were now a good hundred yards into the reservoir at a grand old depth of twelve inches. Our sprint had turned into more of a weak jog. When we finally hit thirteen inches, I decided it was good enough for me. I came to a slow, grinding halt and slid my humbled body down into its thirteen inches of coverage. Others followed my lead and soon all of us were lying flat on our backs on the silt with our heads stuck up at right angles.

The water was cold, the moon bright. We were at least three hundred feet from shore. There was no talking. It appeared all of us were too focused on the return journey to fully enjoy this special moment. I looked across the chilled surface towards my girlfriend. Our eyes met. We both shivered. She smiled weakly back at me and without a single word spoken, we broke up.

3
AMERICA

HIDDEN BEHIND A CLUMP of portly German tourists, Phil Carroll and I watched secretively as the number of Camp America counselors continued to swell. They milled around the British Airways international departure desk at JFK Airport in New York City, each clutching a flimsy, white-paper boarding pass—a clear indicator that their summer in America had drawn to a close. I recognized several faces from our New York-based camp, including Andy McGowan from Glasgow, whose thick Scottish accent was so unintelligible it was as if he spoke a foreign language that only he himself knew; and Simon Long from Sheffield, a lanky, lightly mustachioed nineteen-year-old who had run around the lake each and every morning at breakneck speed.

Ten weeks earlier, I had flown to the United States with hundreds of fresh-faced counselors, all of us eager to teach at summer camps throughout the country. I had never visited the States before and was excited to experience the American way of life. An attractive feature of the program that lured me to sign up with Camp America was that once your camp closed for the season, you had a month to travel on your own before reconvening at JFK to fly back to your normal life in Europe. This hot, late-September day was that day—the end of our American adventure and a scheduled return to normality with a long flight back to the mundane.

Phil Carroll, an athletic, fun-loving twenty-year-old Australian from Sydney, had been an exchange student with a family in Norway when he signed up for the summer escapade; whereas I, at the tender age of twenty-four, had just dissolved my partnership in an estate agency near my home village of Itchenor in the south of England. I had wanted to take some time off to relax and think before jumping into another full-time job.

We had both been assigned positions at Frenchwoods Festival for the Performing Arts—a well-known and respected performing arts camp in upstate New York nestled in the Catskills. Philip's assignment was camp photographer. And me? I was hired to teach the well-known performing art of sailing! Frenchwoods has a private lake with the uninspiring name of Sand Pond, and even though the camp's focus was exclusively on the arts, they just couldn't resist throwing a few Sunfishes, Lasers, and windsurfers into the water. Then, all they had to do was seek out a gullible, foreign sailing instructor from a small sailing village in England to be present on the off chance a fifteen-year-old thespian, in between blocking her role in Annie and attending her advanced tap dance class, might suddenly be overwhelmed with the desire to learn to sail. Needless to say, my summer hadn't been busy—although "Sunbathing on the Boat as Matthew Sailed it Around the Lake 101" did prove to be a popular course for several of the young female campers.

My only success story of the summer was a young boy called Michael. I didn't teach him how to sail, but I did teach him how to say "ready about," "by the lee," and "jibe." Michael oozed with pride when he brought his parents to the water's edge to meet me on Visitors Day. In boisterous nautical fashion, with a distinct theatrical flair and a poorly executed pirate's accent, Michael recited his six sailing-related words. His parents looked at me incredulously, telegraphing that they had expected more bang for their many bucks. I offered a slight shrug. I thought it better not to point out that they had sent their son to a prestigious performing arts camp, an unlikely breeding ground for Olympic yachtsmen.

Once the last camp session ended and the campers had been safely dispatched to their homes across the United States, we were paid our meager salaries in cash and unleashed upon America. The only rule laid out by Camp America was that we were to report to the British Airways departure desk at JFK on September the 22nd by 11:00 a.m.

Phil and I divided our month of travel between Boston, Martha's Vineyard, and New York City, staying with friends we'd made during our time at the camp. Our whirlwind northeast tour had been liberally punctuated with beaches, barbeques, bars, baseball games, parties, laughter, and revelry.

At 10:55 a.m., still obscured by our German cover, Phil looked at me and said matter-of-factly, "I'm having too much fun in America. You?" I glanced at the mass of counselors who were now five minutes away from terminating their American sojourn.

"Yes," I whispered. "Yes, I am," I repeated more confidently, as if confirming to myself that I had indeed just said yes and that yes was indeed the correct answer. Phil's brand new Boston Red Sox cap (a purchase he regretted a year later when Bill Buckner's infamous blunder robbed the Sox of a 1986 World Series title), pulled down snugly, hid all but his unblinking eyes. I froze.

Everything around me seemed still and quiet. Seconds elongated. I felt as if I'd left the airport and transported to a library. The threat of being aggressively hushed by a stern librarian was palpable. The enormity of the choice we were contemplating yawned before us. Crouched down with our backpacks and sleeping bags next to us, without the slightest hint of fear, Phil said as evenly as if reciting a password, "Let's jump ship."

"Done," I responded. I didn't hesitate. I didn't question. I committed 100% to the idea. I grabbed my measly belongings and kept my head down as I slipped quietly away from certainty, obligations, and my homeland.

I knew instinctively where we were heading. Eight weeks earlier we had met Roberta when she had been visiting Frenchwoods from her home in Dallas, Texas.

During the wee hours of the morning at a local Hancock, New York bar, through a Genesee-Cream-Ale-induced haze, Roberta had vaguely suggested that if Phil and I stayed in America beyond September we could maybe paint her house in the fall. "Wee hours of the morning," "ale-induced haze," "vaguely" and "maybe" are not words or phrases on which to base a life-changing decision. But nothing can take away from the fact that in that split second in the airport everything became crystal clear. I never had any doubt that this was the correct decision. I couldn't verbalize it, but it just felt right.

I have always thought it a little disturbing that I often make decisions in this rather intuitive way, until I stumbled across an article about the human brain in *The New Yorker*. It explained that the oldest and deepest parts of my brain, while responsible for feelings and behavior and for controlling decision-making, have no capacity for language. So it became clear to me that when I make decisions purely on gut instinct, it is naturally rather challenging for me to put my rationale into words. Before learning this, I had always thought that I simply possessed an alarmingly high comfort level with the grey areas of life, which was coupled with an exceptionally large dose of plain ol' good luck.

As a boy in England, I distinctly remember my lucky rabbit's foot key ring. Regularly, I pulled it out and stroked the soft fur in hopes of prolonging what I thought was my lucky streak of random decision-making. I confess that as a boy I always struggled to justify how an object that was reputed to bring me good luck had so obviously brought such cripplingly bad luck to the unfortunate donor of the foot. While stroking my lucky rabbit's foot, it was impossible for me to block out the image of the hobbled rabbit to which the appendage once belonged. I imagined his ears laid back and nose wrinkled up in disdain while pointing an accusatory paw directly at me and grumbling caustically, "Next time cut off your own damn foot, Motherfucker." In retrospect, the only "luck" associated with this ill-conceived charm was that I eventually lost it and no longer had to be subjected to the guilt or the scarring images of a bitter, crippled, and foul-mouthed rabbit.

We exited the international terminal and stood up straight and tall for the first time in an hour, proud to be seen. Every step my fully-functional feet took, distancing me further from the British Airways departure desk, made me tingle with excitement. I felt almost American as we strode towards domestic departures.

I looked confidently at the congenial, smartly uniformed ticket lady standing behind the People's Express ticket counter and said, "Two tickets to Dallas, Texas please."

"And when will you be returning, sir?"

"Never," we replied in unison.

I presented my nearly-maxed-out credit card. She held up her neatly manicured hand to stop me.

"Here at People's Express, sir, you pay on the plane. It will be $69 each."

"Wonderful," I said, slipping my weary credit card back into the safety of my wallet.

Sure enough, somewhere over Kentucky, in between my small, fifty-cent packet of peanuts and a Diet Coke, a flight attendant arrived at my seat with a rickety, manual credit card machine and crunched the $69 out of my Visa. The transaction was complete. My life had leaped forward in yet another unexpected twist. Now, I just had to keep up and make a quick adjustment to the game plan.

As I sat on the plane, I considered how my life best resembled a giant game of Pong, where I was the ball but I also controlled the paddles. I bounced from one adventure to another. Sometimes, I moved slowly while carefully adjusting the paddles to stay in control. Then, with little warning, life picked up and off I went at breakneck speed, ricocheting off people, places, and ideas at obtuse angles—barely able to stay in the game. Occasionally, I careened off the screen altogether. While out of view, I would catch my breath, regroup, and serve myself again. Life was an exciting game to play, and all I needed was some time, a few quarters, and a willingness to press "start."

Upon leaving the plane, it felt as if we had inadvertently happened upon the set of *True Grit*. I stood and marveled. As a boy growing up in England, I had regularly played cowboys and fondly remember receiving a cowboy outfit at Christmas when I was eight years old. I spent many hours riding my imaginary range, wearing my black cowboy hat, fringed pleather waistcoat with my trusty cardboard holster, and shiny six-shooter on my side, but I'd never seen people wearing real cowboy hats, boots, and oversized belt buckles as their everyday clothing.

The Wrangler jeans rep for the Dallas area must have been a very wealthy man. I could not help but notice many of his customers moseying down the concourse with slightly bowed legs, as if they'd just gotten off their horses and sauntered right into the airport. I wondered if Hertz, Budget, and Alamo's rental offerings included full-size, mid-size, and palomino. When people spoke, their southern Texas drawl mesmerized me—warm and slow, it drew me in. I noticed them adding additional syllables, which ran words together and created a continuous rhythmic flow that gently washed over me, welcoming me to the Lone Star State.

There was no mistaking that we had arrived in Texas. The problem was that no one in the state of Texas knew we had arrived. Phil and I strolled over to the bank of payphones lining the wall, matching as best we could the slow, wide-legged strides of the locals.

As I approached the phone closest to us I thought, *Why didn't we call Roberta prior to actually flying all the way to Dallas? If she happens to be on vacation or doesn't remember us, we have absolutely no backup plan.* Roberta was the only person Phil and I knew in the entire state of Texas, and Texas, we'd heard, was big—at least two times the size of England.

Two reasons sprang to mind for why we had not called Roberta prior to our arrival. First, it would be a lot easier for her to say no if she knew we had a safe, secure, and well-thought-out backup plan, such as a prepaid flight back to England. Second, our adventurous spirits.

I rummaged through a side pocket of my backpack, eventually producing a crumpled piece of napkin with the name "Roberta" and a ten-digit number scrawled across it in drunken penmanship. I lifted the receiver, deposited a dime, and dialed. A second later I heard, "Hello, this is Roberta." *So far, so good,* I thought.

"Hi. This is Matthew," I said in the cheery tone reserved exclusively for people who are about to ask for a huge favor. There was no response. I quickly added, "Matthew Taylor?" Still silence. "Matthew Taylor and Phil? From Frenchwoods?" More silence. My heart rate soared as the pitch of my voice rose to an almost girlish tone. "We met this summer?"

"Ah, yes," said Roberta as she pieced it together. "How are you guys?"

"Great," I exhaled. "Great," I repeated to buy me time to think of how to pose the next, rather important question. Feeling uncreative, I decided not to beat about the bush. "This summer you had sort of mentioned we could maybe paint your house this fall. We were just wondering how serious you were about that."

"Where are you?"

"Dallas Airport."

"Oh." She paused for what seemed like minutes and then said quite happily, "I'll send my son to pick you up. He'll be there in about twenty minutes."

"Brilliant. Thanks."

I hung up, looked at Phil, smiled, and said, "That was easy."

Twenty minutes later, true to her word, a silver sporty Mitsubishi Starion screeched to a halt at passenger pickup. The door swung open. As we started to climb in, Roberta's son, Rob, leaned towards us—his lightly-stubbled, smiling face peeked from beneath a pristine black cowboy hat. A gigantic belt buckle dominated his midsection, covering a large portion of his perfectly pressed western shirt, creating the appearance of him having little to no torso. A brand new pair of tight-fitting Wrangler jeans and a well-worn, but highly polished, pair of Roper boots completed the look for what had to be the quintessential urban cowboy.

Rob greeted us with a cheery, "Howdy," then handed us a welcome basket in the shape of an ice-cold twelve-pack of Coors Light. Phil and I popped open a couple of cans. Under my breath I muttered, "Giddy up," as we squealed away from the curb like a silver bullet. Unbeknownst to me, in that moment of intuitive, wild abandon, I had just emigrated.

4
CARPOOL

SHE WAITED PATIENTLY in front of my house as the sun bathed her in warmth. Light created a misty glow around her. She was beautiful. I'd never experienced this kind of attraction before. *Was I dreaming? Could this really be happening to me?* I blinked, then shut my eyes and ever so slowly allowed them to open. I was sure she would be gone, my dream over, and my life returned to normal. But there she remained, ready and willing to change my life forever. My first company car.

And what a car she was! A sleek, sexy, fast, powerful Ferrari-red beast. At least that is how I viewed her. To the trained eye of an experienced car salesman, a more accurate description would be a secondhand 1979 red Vauxhall Cavalier. But she was mine, all mine. I was proud of her, and we had an instant affection for each other.

Being twenty-two and having never owned a car before, I was not the only person excited by this circumstance. The many friends who'd spent the previous five years carting me around the English countryside from pub to pub or pub to party or party to pub were also ecstatic at the prospect of having another designated driver, especially one who owed a lot of favors.

We'd all been invited by a friend of a friend of a friend to a Sunday lunchtime garden party in Bosham. I decided there was no time like the present to begin returning those favors. I called Neal, then Roger, and quickly arranged pickup times. They seemed thrilled that I was now in the position to jeopardize my license for a change.

Sunday morning arrived and along with it came sunshine, which is a huge bonus for a garden party but never a guarantee in England. I strutted like a peacock towards my company car. I pulled open her door and slid into paradise. The smell of Armor-All, hot vinyl, and stale cigarette smoke greeted me. A turn of the key brought the engine to life. I glanced at the rudimentary arrangement of dials and gauges and accelerated smoothly away, the eleven hundred cubic centimeter engine laboring to keep up with my expectations.

Cars were so necessary for us because we all lived around the Chichester Channel. It's a beautiful part of southern England. The ancient Roman city of Chichester sits eight miles inland. Between it and the south coast is the Chichester Channel, which starts at the Solent and meanders its way inland, every now and then splitting and creating a watery finger that ripples its way deep into the countryside. At the end of every finger is a classic English sailing village, each with a classic English sailing village name such as Itchenor, Birdham, Emsworth, Dell Quay, and Bosham. Every village in turn has its own sailing club, church, pub, a few stores, and beautiful homes worth a king's ransom, offering glorious views across the watery landscapes. The distance between each village as the crow flies is minimal; to get to them without wings, you have to drive around the furthest tips of each inlet.

I lived in Itchenor. If you follow Itchenor Road to the village, it will take you past the church, the Ship Inn, the turn to the sailing club, and, ultimately, straight into the water. If you look across the water, there is Bosham, scarcely a mile away, but by car it's a twelve-mile journey through winding English lanes where you often spend time behind the inevitable tractor or an elderly gentleman crawling along in a Morris 1000 with a tweed hat on the back shelf.

I drew up outside Neal's apartment and for the first time honked my horn. I was surprised at how robust it sounded. Neal and Roger tumbled out of the front door laughing, their faces beaming with mischievousness. Both were wearing blue blazers, jeans, and crumpled white dress shirts. Neal beat Roger to the front seat and settled in.

"Well, well, well," he said cheerily. "I never thought I'd see this day. Taylor has a car. Come on, then, let's go."

I jerkily pulled out, almost stalling the car, much to the amusement of my passengers. We were off and on our way to Bosham.

I knew we were getting close as I turned onto Smugglers Lane, which runs parallel to the water's edge. All the gardens of the houses to our left ran straight down to the water. Most had their own private jetties with sleek yachts rocking gently against their moorings. The excess of motor vehicles identified the correct home. I drew into the driveway, and even the scrunch of the thick gravel sounded upmarket. We parked and climbed out into another world. Roger and Neal stood in silence as they took in the view while subconsciously running their hands up and down the fronts of their crinkled shirts in a belated attempt to iron them.

The monstrous two-hundred-year-old home stood proudly amidst its perfectly proportioned gardens. Ivy grew up the red brick walls and over the exposed beams. The open five-car garage revealed a who's who in Italian and German sports cars. The only non-sporty representative was a Bentley. The lawns to each side of the home were dark green, cut short, and ran all the way down to the sea wall. Flower beds exploded with color. Dotted over the lawns were white tents housing buffet tables laden with succulent food and bars offering the very best liquor.

The hundreds of guests sauntered about exuding an air of entitlement. All were decked out in traditional garden party garb—flowing floral dresses topped with elaborate hats, blue blazers with white pants, and even the occasional straw boater.

A summer breeze carried the smell of salt, the caw of seagulls, and the unending slapping of halyards on masts. This was a true English summer garden party being hosted in an idyllic setting on the water's edge of an exclusive West Sussex sailing village. It was as if we were walking into an issue of *Vanity Fair*.

We gathered our wits and headed to the lawn in search of one tent in particular. It was easy to spot, even though it was smaller and off to the side, as if the host had been trying to hide it. What made it unmistakable was the large number of people gathered around it and the din they created. This garden party had promised to be different in one respect. They were serving kegs of real ale, which in all honestly just isn't a good idea.

For those who have never had a brush with real ale, here's a little information. It's ale, which as far as I can tell is a posh name for beer that's been brewed in wooden kegs without carbonation by individual pubs in small quantities with no governmental controls. The results are startling—an amazing variety of tastes, colors, and weights with only one consistent factor, an exceptionally high alcohol content. The first pint slips down effortlessly and is usually accompanied by much chitchat about the ale's various qualities and style. "Mm ... delicious. Quite light, this one. I might have another. Let's get these down, shall we?" The second one slides down a little slower, but still with great enthusiasm—certainly enough to cover up the fact that your fine motor skills have started to fail.

After the third pint, those who aren't regular drinkers start to experience a sudden, awkward loss of major limb control. Priceless family heirlooms begin to get knocked over as an arm, for example, inexplicably flaps like the wing of an albatross, destroying all in its path. This is instantly followed by an overly detailed apology along the lines of, "Oh-goodness-gracious. Sorry, silly old me, clumsy old fool, my fault. I'm sure you can get another from IKEA. Silly place for it really. I'll get a cloth. Anyone need another drink?" It never seems to suffice to just say, "Sorry, I'm drunk."

The fourth pint is never a smart decision, and it is at this point, for all but true professional drinkers, that the "garden" part of the party will suddenly and without warning rise up to meet you. There is nothing in this world less sophisticated than a crumpled body, loosely connected to a floral dress, sprawled across a well-manicured lawn. Real ale is dangerous. It's not something to be trifled with, which is why the vast majority of the world wisely chooses to drink less-real ale, or even pretend ale (also known as Budweiser).

Over the next three-and-a-half hours, we proceeded to experience the wonders of real ale and its powerful effects on the general population. I tried my best to be responsible since I had the keys to the Scarlet Beauty, while Neal and Roger didn't try very hard at all. As the party was drawing to a sloppy close, I rounded up my boisterous passengers. We weaved our way up the lawn towards my car, receiving along the way several slurred farewells delivered in a variety of upper-class English accents. Neal had invited two friends to travel with us. Real ale had made both Nick and Paul extremely jolly and rendered them utterly incapable of operating their own motor vehicles. The doors of my Vauxhall Cavalier slammed shut, sealing the five of us in.

"Brilliant party!" bellowed Neal.

"Bloody great, really top notch," Roger agreed enthusiastically. "I can't believe the real ale never ran out."

"I did my best to help them," shared Paul.

"I think we all should be very proud of our consumption," laughed Neal. "Here Taylor, do you want a cigarette?"

"No, thanks," I replied absentmindedly. I was more concerned about how hard I needed to concentrate behind the wheel of my car. I felt okay, but the effect of the ale was lingering. They lit cigarettes and away we drove in a rollicking, smoke-filled, beery haze.

We had a choice for our return trip. We could either return to the main road (the quicker inland way) or go the scenic route following the water's edge all the way to the village. Without consultation, I opted for the scenic route. A good rule regarding scenic byways, however, is to go on them only if you are confident all of the vehicle's occupants are really interested in the scenery.

The road to Bosham is beautiful; it's a narrow lane barely wide enough for one car. It meanders alongside the Bosham Channel, following the random twists and turns nature has made as the water cuts its way inland. The ever-present breeze dances playfully across the rippled surface of the water and carries the wonderful salty smell of the sea. At low tide, the salty smell is overpowered by the pungent odor of wet mudflats and seaweed.

As you near the village of Bosham, the road starts to make a large loop around the head of the inlet. This is one of the most famous parts of the Chichester Channel for two reasons. First, if you look across the small inlet to Bosham, it's as if you are looking at a postcard that's come to life. It is an image that has appeared in countless books and magazines. Boats of all shape and size tug gently at their moorings, their bows pointing in the same direction, slaves to the power of the tide. Across the water, hundred-year-old cottages with mottled tile roofs of various pitches line the water's edge—guarded against the ever-present saltwater by stone walls. An ancient steeple points towards the heavens. A thatched cottage with whitewashed walls, a pub, and a sailing club perched at the tip of the landmass, its piers and jetties offering a link between the land and sea. All the ingredients for a perfect sailing village are present and correct, set under a blue sky with some well-placed fluffy white clouds.

Second, this is where King Canute reputedly placed his throne on the shore, and with all his royal might, commanded the incoming tide to stop. It did not, which proved the king's point—his immense power paled in comparison to the power of God.

Every now and then there is a hump in the road. These are caused by large drainage pipes that run under the road and allow the fields on the right to drain. To the left are nothing but sailboats, birds, water, and mud-flats—the proportions of each depend upon the state of the tide.

Apparently, another feature of real ale is that it diminishes one's ability to enjoy sightseeing. The amount of interest my companions now had in the scenery was nil. This was in stark contrast to the excessive amount of interest possessed by the carload of tourists in front of us. They proceeded to crawl along between two and four miles per hour the entire way. As we drove, trapped behind them, I watched as seagulls to our left and an assortment of farm animals to our right easily outpaced us. To inflict yet more pain, the car in front insisted on coming to a complete stop on top of every drainage pipe, as if the gain of two feet in elevation afforded the occupants an entirely different view.

After the car in front passed the second lay-by, where the driver could easily have drawn over and allowed us to pass, the frustration among my real-ale-fueled passengers hit a fevered pitch. The first audible cries of indignation were contained within the vehicle, but as soon as both cars came to a grinding halt after another arduous two-foot assent and eventual summit of Mt. Drainage Pipe, my windows descended en masse. The encouragement to move on was not subtle. When it was met with no response, my passengers reverted to a technique I call "An Englishman in Europe." That is to say, when a foreigner does not understand your perfect King's English, one can assume that he clearly didn't hear you. A simple increase in volume works flawlessly.

The volume increased...substantially. And to add dramatic effect, Neal and Paul felt it necessary to deliver their personal diatribes with the upper halves of their bodies thrust completely out of the car windows, ably accompanied by Roger, who was leaning across me to depress the horn for five-second spells at a time.

As the only reasonably sober person, this was all a bit too much for me to bear, and I sank down behind my wheel, hoping the harassed driver would choose to move on quickly. He did not. What he did do was rather surprising. He got out of his car and walked briskly towards us. Upon arrival at my door, he stuck his head through my open window and bellowed at the top of his lungs, "I don't know if you boys have been drinking or ..." He stopped, instantly engulfed by the pungency created when real ale is consumed with vigor. He coughed and sputtered. For a millisecond he seemed confused; the result, perhaps, of the impressive smolder having gotten the better of him. Then he leapt into action. His right hand darted into my car and grabbed the keys, yanking them out of the ignition. Holding them up as he retreated speedily to his own car, he yelled in a broad cockney accent, "I'm taking these to the police station." His short, rounded body waddled briskly back to his car. Heavy gold chains around his neck swung side to side. I noticed as he disappeared into his car that the thick black hair from his broad back curled up and over the neckline of his sweatshirt, as if he were a bear cross-dressing as a man.

We sat in stunned silence, each of us grappling with the humbling fact that when confronted with a key stealing crisis, we did absolutely nothing. I had to commend this tourist for his bold and decisive action. Unfortunately, I would have to criticize him as well for his lack of local knowledge.

It took a minute for it to sink in, and then the gravity of the situation became abundantly clear. My two-day-old beloved company car, complete with steering wheel lock, was stranded on a tiny Bosham road while some random tourist was delivering my keys to some random police station. Clearly, he was completely oblivious to the fact that in an hour and twenty minutes the road would be under four feet of saltwater. Yes, with each and every high tide, the Bosham road floods.

When someone says, "That was sobering," I wonder if that person has actually experienced the phenomenon. I can vouch for five people who have. We all got out of the car without a word. Some looked at the car. Some looked at the water. The ones looking at the rising water looked away hopelessly. Every ripple pushed its way up the shore, surpassing the previous ripple's effort in an unstoppable advance upon my car. I felt a distinct kinship with King Canute.

A plan had to be hatched and hatched fast. This was our chance to redeem ourselves from our previous dismal performance when confronted with crisis. It felt good to take action. Eagerly, we assessed the situation. The car was in the middle of the road, but luckily the front wheels were angled away from the water. Even with the steering lock on, we could push the car in an arc away from the fast approaching water to as far as the seawall. This would buy us some time.

We assumed that the car keys would ultimately fall into the hands of the police, but where? This presented a greater problem. As much as I had shown restraint at the garden party, my restraint had been a little halfhearted. In the cold light of day I had to admit that if breathalyzed the likelihood was that I would fail, thus complicating the already complicated situation. If the police were to show up with my keys and give them to me, and if I were to then drive my car to safety, would they then proceed to breathalyze me and take my license? It was at this point we conjured the Master Plan. Even though it seemed a little English for my tastes, it was unanimously accepted and immediately implemented.

First, we pushed my car so that the front bumper was touching the seawall. Then, we looked across the water to the picturesque village of Bosham and the building upon which our plan depended.

The plan was this: We would walk as fast as we could to the pub. Upon arrival at the Anchor Bleu, I would proceed to drink two pints of bitter and a double scotch in front of the landlord (the owner of the pub). This way if the police did arrive with my keys, I could say I was so worried and distraught about my car and the overreacting tourist that I had had a few drinks and I was now worried I might be over the limit. Plus, I would have the landlord as a witness to say I'd drunk more than the legal limit at his pub. The police could then send someone else to move the car, but they wouldn't be able to prove I had been over the limit at the time of the incident. We had hatched a clever and cunning plan.

With one final glance at the ever-rising water, we knew we had no time to waste. We set off at a good clip with the Anchor Bleu as our windward mark. Twenty minutes later, red-faced and sweaty, we crossed the threshold of the historic pub. Moments after that, I stood in front of a slightly puzzled landlord, a pint in each hand and a double scotch on the nearby bar. I bashed both pints and made short work of the scotch. The plan was working to perfection, except for one slight flaw. I was beginning to feel the side effects of the plan. My urgency to act was wilting. Neal bought a round of drinks and included me just to make absolutely certain I was over the limit. I was positive the police would show up at the Anchor Bleu. The idea was not that farfetched. In England, a large amount of petty crimes are solved in or around the pub. We settled into a table by the window with a clear view of my car across the inlet.

The water was starting to creep across the road, edging its way closer and closer to the object of my affections. Even if the police arrived right now, it would be too late to save her. I had nothing to do except sit and watch the flooding of my car. Word of our predicament spread quickly through the pub. As the water rose, so did the level of interest and sympathy. Drinks started to appear from all over the pub, often accompanied by a rough slap on the back or simple words of encouragement such as, "It's all right, mate, it'll dry out."

We dutifully accepted all the drinks since we didn't want to dampen the spirits of our new friends, plus those drinks were certainly easing my pain. People jostled for positions at the windows, and when the water first touched the tires of my car, a hearty cheer went up and was accompanied by a round of applause. A flurry of drinks followed. Now everybody in the pub was involved; even people outside on the street were abreast of the situation. Drinks flew around. People traded out time at the windows while a fellow named Tyg kept us all informed of the progress with a live running commentary. I was the host of a Come-Watch-My-Car-Get-Flooded-Party and it was a huge hit.

The water lapped at the tires. It was as if the Anchor Bleu was about to win the FA Cup Final. People went wild. So much so that no one heard the old sea dog sitting back in a dark corner. He wore a charcoal-gray knitted sweater that blended into his silvery beard. His unkempt hair was slightly nicotine-stained, his face weather-beaten and creased, yet his blue eyes twinkled with the knowledge of the sea. His thick hands, rounded and calloused, clutched a filterless French cigarette; the smoke casually curled its way up through his beard and into his hair.

He spoke again. "You be a lucky bastard, lad. It's the neeps right now."

"What was that?" I asked.

"It's the neeps tides right now. Neeps. The lowest tides of the year."

"Thank you," I said, "Thank you."

I ran to the window. I didn't want to be the bearer of bad news and dampen the fervor of my party. So I just watched and prayed. The water level was now just below the sills of the doors; another inch and I would be officially sunk. I held my breath. The water held steady. It didn't seem to be rising. I noticed people starting to drift away from the windows, a little despondent that they didn't get the full submersion they had been banking on. I stared out of the window in silence and, sure enough, the water started to recede five minutes later. I felt strangely superior to King Canute.

My car was saved! Time to celebrate! Roger was quick to supply a liquid celebration. Relief swept over me and the tension eased out of my body. Finally able to relax, I now realized just how shitfaced I was. I decided to take it easy for a while as my colleagues continued making merry. I drifted outside to get some fresh air and watch the glorious sunset over the waters of Bosham Channel and my brand new company car.

Much refreshed from my break and with dusk upon me, I realized it was time for action. I walked back into the pub to let the guys know I was heading down the street to the phone box to call the police. They were thrilled to hear that the saga continued.

After a two-minute stroll, I found myself standing in front of the telephone box. There are few things as iconic as a good old-fashioned British telephone box—painted bright Royal Mail red from top to bottom, standing at attention, rigid as a guard, with seventy-two small glass panes and an inscription of the bleeding obvious just above the door: TELEPHONE.

I pulled open the door and stepped into the familiar and unmistakable faint scent of urine and vomit. One gravitates to a phone box when extremely drunk, because once inside their cozy confines it is impossible to fall over, unless you crumple like an imploding building and collapse straight down inside yourself.

I looked up the number for the local cop shop, took a deep breath, and dialed. Immediately, I heard a voice.

"Bosham Police Station."

"Hello," I said cheerily, "I was driving this afternoon and—"

I stopped in mid-sentence because someone had opened the door behind me. I spun around and there occupying the entire space where the door had been loomed a large policeman. You can imagine my shock at the efficiency of their service. He stood there, a pillar of society, blocking my way out; but he was also sealing in my beer-reeking breath. For a moment, I wished the smell of pee and vomit was stronger.

My mother's voice echoed in my head. "Remember dear, you never have a second chance to make a first impression." I know I was expected to do something, but what? I was still stunned and confused by his timely arrival, so I just sheepishly handed him the phone and said feebly, "It's for you." I stepped out. He stepped in.

"Hello?" he said quizzically into the phone. Then a second later he said, "Oh, George, okay, mate, I'll take it from 'ere. Cheers, then." He hung up.

The giant policeman stepped out of the phone box, looked straight at me, and said, "I bet you're looking for your keys." I smiled weakly. "Yes," I said.

"Well it's good news for you, I 'ave um 'ere. 'Op in. I'll run you out to your car."

I hopped in. Of course the many beers and double scotch I had consumed at the Anchor Blue came along for the ride as well. So I now sat next to a police officer who was driving me to my car where he would hand me my keys. I would then jump in, start her up, move two feet, and he'd pull me over and charge me (quite rightly) for driving under the influence. I decided I would go on the offensive before this scenario became reality. Talking through my teeth with my lips completely shut, as if I were a ventriloquist, in an attempt to prevent my beery breath from leaking out, I said, "What wiff the tooist overreacting and the worry of my new car, I've had a few drinks to calm the nerves. I wonder if I'll be okay to dreeve?"

He replied, "Oh, a couple of drinks never 'urt anyone."

And that was that. We arrived. He handed me my keys and said, "Just follow me back to town and have a good one, mate." I said, "Thanks."

It was as if nothing had happened. My precious car was completely unharmed. I climbed in and she started first time. I was home free. All I had to do was not draw attention to myself with any erratic driving. I took a deep breath, told myself to focus, and eased the car forward.

Everything was going swimmingly until all of a sudden I felt the backend of my car start to slip sideways. I turned the wheel in the opposite direction and corrected the skid, but as soon as I accelerated the back lost traction and skidded again. I thought to myself, "Wow, I really shouldn't be driving." I peered out of the windscreen wondering if the policeman in front was noticing that I was having a problem keeping my car in a straight line. I lightly accelerated and again the rear slipped out. It was then I noticed the road surface. Illuminated by my headlights, the entire road appeared green. When the tide had come in, it brought seaweed with it, and when it receded, the seaweed was left high and wet, covering the road with three inches of a slippery green coating. Relieved that it wasn't just my impaired state that was causing me to struggle, I proceeded to slip and slide my way back to Bosham.

Upon arrival, my police escort peeled off to the right and disappeared. I found a parking spot and reentered the Anchor Bleu to find the rest of my party in fine form. I walked up to their table and held my car keys high above my head. The gesture was greeted with a huge roar of approval. As the volume died down, I smiled and proclaimed, "My round! It's time to celebrate!"

5
FROG

THE MORNING WE SPRINKLED my mother's ashes, the Highlands of Scotland dressed for the occasion in her most rare attire: crystal clear blue skies brimming with golden sunshine cascading down from the heavens. The day was glorious.

My mother Sylvia had come to my sister Jessica's guesthouse in Scotland to recuperate from chemotherapy less than two months earlier. But the cancer would not rest and callously stole our mother from us before she ever had a chance to return home to England. She had always loved Scotland, so we decided to gather there to pay our last respects.

I pushed open the heavy front door of the small guesthouse and ventured outside. Nature's magnificence bombarded my senses. The sun's warm fingers curled around me and gently eased the sadness from my body.

The fresh smell of the saturated grass and shrubs lifted me as my eyes attempted to distinguish the staggering multitude of shades of green. A rare perfect day in the Highlands.

Once we arrived at the funeral home, our small group of Mum's immediate family piled out of four cars and walked along a winding path past meticulously manicured hedges and up a few wide shallow steps to the Garden of Remembrance. It was an unfamiliar journey, one only traveled by those off to sprinkle…or to remember.

The garden was much larger than I expected—more like a Field of Remembrance. I instantly liked its wide open natural state. A distinct slope imparted the permanent feeling of listing. If you looked down the slope to the east, the waters of the Bule Firth shimmered in the distance beyond the city of Inverness.

On any less somber occasion, the lush emerald grass would have welcomed us to run barefoot. Reflections from the morning sunlight danced and flickered amongst our feet. Every blade was topped by its own individual drop of dew, as if they had all shown up to a party wearing the same hat. It seemed to be a very nice place to sprinkle ashes. If I *had* to sprinkle ashes.

Like many Brits, we stood in a little group and talked mindlessly about the weather, shuttering our true feelings. Within a few minutes my mother's remains arrived, brought to us by two gentlemen wearing blue lab coats with Inverness Crematorium embroidered on the pocket.

They handed Mum's ashes to the minister and retreated to a safe distance away.

The minister then asked us where we would like to sprinkle the ashes. This, I confess, caught me a bit off guard. Here we stood in a large field with my mother's ashes contained in a sprinkling device, and suddenly we were expected to make a decision. Was one spot in this vast expanse of green better than another? Would Mother have a preference? I could picture Sylvia up there, looking down as the first ashes hit the green, green grass, putting her hands to either side of her slowly shaking head and saying in a disappointed tone, "Not there."

I was a little hesitant. So were my fellow mourners. There was a little oohing and ahhing, a few helpless facial expressions, and then the decision was made. It appeared, as luck would have it, that the very place where we were all standing would be the perfect spot after all. Then the minister asked who would like to sprinkle Mother first.

I had never been to one of these events before, so possibly I could be excused for not having thoroughly thought it through. I understood that the ashes would be dispersed, but I never really thought that I would be a disperser. I just assumed it would be somebody else's job.

Nobody looked overly excited about taking on the task. There stood the minister holding Mum, with a "come on folks, let's get this show rolling" look on his face, while all of us stood around awkwardly shuffling our feet and muttering to each other, exhibiting another popular Britishism—being overly polite.

"After you."

"No, no couldn't possibly, Old Chap, after you."

"No, no, no I insist, after you."

How the hell we ever ended up with an Empire I'll never know.

Eventually, my sister Jessica reluctantly stepped forward. The minister handed her the sprinkling device.

The urn was gold in color, bulbous at the bottom with a handle extending upwards. Under the handle was a small lever, which you pulled up to release the ashes out of the base. There must have been a circular bottom that was pulled up, because the ashes poured out on all sides and formed a circle, similar to a fertilizer dispenser. I watched my sister sprinkle with great aplomb, and then it was my turn.

There are so few certainties in life. Even life itself is one big uncertainty, except for the fact that at some point it will end. Here I was at the certain point of my mother's life, and yet even that now proved to present uncertainties for those of us who were left behind. What exactly was in this golden bulbous urn? Was it all Mum and nothing else? What about the coffin? Was that in there, too? If so, what is the average person-to-coffin-ratio in your run-of-the-mill cremation? Is a simple list of ingredients too much to ask for?

I am sure the only reason these frivolous thoughts flooded my mind was because I knew my sisters and I were all very secure in the knowledge that my mother's spirit had long since flown with the angels to a most beautiful, peaceful place. No fear surrounded my mother's death. There had been of course immense sadness, tears, long silent loving looks, the clasping of a frail bony hand that had once lifted me up effortlessly to sweep me away from danger, internal nagging questions such as *Why?*, the gazing at old photographs, the touching of familiar rings, necklaces, and brooches, the retelling of stories, small glasses of sherry, moments of laughter, more tears, and Mother's occasional reprimand. But, thank God, there had never been any fear.

We certainly didn't all share the same religious beliefs, but we all had faith. For me to confront death without some form of faith would make for a very lonely day. Faith, however much it challenges me, is the easier option.

Coming to terms with my mother's absence proved to be my greater struggle. I could no longer touch her hand, hear her voice, or see her. There was no place for me to mail a birthday card. I desperately needed some form of closure to allow me to move on.

My usual response to confronting the confusions of life is to pigeon-hole them. Or to put it another way, I conveniently place them in boxes. I discovered I confront death in a similar, simplistic way. The box can be buried. The box can be burned. Sprinkling my mother's ashes proved to be my release, my final farewell to the physical.

Apart from my somewhat unnecessary preoccupation as to what I was actually sprinkling, I now felt haunted with a much greater concern. As I helped my seven-year-old daughter Maitland and five-year-old son Alastair with their sprinkling duties, uneasiness swept over me. I realized that there was potential for committing what would have to be considered one of the world's greatest faux pas: to sprinkle the last of the ashes and not leave a serving of Mother for another guest.

My mind raced to Christmas dinners where we halved and halved again the smallest bit of mashed potatoes so as not to become that greedy, unmannered, inconsiderate pig who gobbled up the last portion. That was just mashed potatoes. This was my mother!

The urn itself was heavy; combined with my inexperience as a sprinkler there was just no way to tell how much of Mother was left to go around. Perhaps a small gauge on the side of the urn with an orange needle and a well-marked "F" and "E" would have been a nice touch. As it was, the ashes might just peter out at any moment, leaving an eager-to-sprinkle second cousin ashless, heartbroken, and bitter.

With this immense risk looming over me, I erred quite understandably on the cautious side. A little sprinkle here, a little sprinkle there. All parties who participated did likewise, and this left us with a somewhat different dilemma—a bit too much of Mum to go around. Everybody had sprinkled and there was still a considerable amount of Mother left.

As we were all crippled by our ignorance of ash sprinkling protocol, I took it upon myself to finish the job and this time gave it a bit of what-for. There was something quite freeing knowing that my goal was to simply sprinkle every last glorious ash. I decided to enjoy it. Throwing Mother to the wind, I created elaborate patterns while spinning the urn at such a dizzying speed I must have looked like a whirling Dervish.

Eventually, like all good things, she came to an end. After I handed the urn back to the minister, a still, peaceful, loving silence followed. And with it, the sobering realization that my mother was physically gone forever.

The beautiful silence was quickly shattered by one of Mother's six grandchildren shouting excitedly, "It's a frog! It's a frog!" The grandchildren quickly surrounded the vulnerable amphibian, and my son wasted no time with a speedy capture.

There we stood in a field in Scotland. The adults in quiet tearful reflection. The children excitedly examining the many attributes of a small shimmering frog.

One by one, the adults felt a pull towards the children's group and drifted quietly over to the livelier circle. Let's be honest, a live two-inch frog held in the hand of a live five-year-old boy is a far more alluring attraction than a few sprinkled ashes. As I wandered over with a smile on my face and tears in my eyes, I marveled at how precious life is and how I have a responsibility to live and celebrate every moment of it.

I looked down at my son's tiny hand carefully holding the frog and an odd notion popped into my mind.

It couldn't be.

Could it?

I looked closely at the frog and then with my lips barely moving, I whispered, "Mum?"

6
POPPING THE QUESTION

Hidden in a plate of food at an elegant restaurant.
Attached to the collar of a favorite pet.
Camouflaged by flowers.
Housed in a box made entirely of Belgian chocolate.
Submerged in Dom Perignon.

DESPITE THE SOPHISTICATION of subterfuge, the significance of the engagement ring remains the same: an invitation to join in a union for life.

Six months after Susan Hennessy first waited on my table at the 14th Street Bar & Grill in Boulder I knew she was the one. I loved her effervescent spirit, cherubic face, and a laugh so loud and distinct that even in a large crowd I always felt she was nearby.

Six months after Susan delivered that bowl of carrot and cumin soup, she knew I was the one. Her illustration of this point was clear. Each and every day she posed the question, "Do you have anything important to ask me?" I did, but I couldn't just blurt out, "Will you marry me?" I wanted to plan a memorable proposal even though planning has never been my strong suit. It ended up being another three months before I popped the question.

I didn't want to risk losing my future bride during my planning period, so I felt it best to take up the challenge and always have a question ready to ask her. That's ninety-one "important questions" I had to come up with prior to, "Will you marry me?" As I approached the high seventies, I noticed the quality of my important questions beginning to wane.

Question 78: Who *did* let the dogs out?

Susan is the youngest of eight girls. That's eight girls all born within a span of nine years. Two decades later, this equated to one wedding every one-and-one-eighth years. It's no surprise Susan's father was still working full-time at age eighty.

The fourth eldest Hennessy, Stacy, was getting married that same summer in New York City. The whole family would be present. During the early part of the weekend I planned to collar Susan's dad (perhaps after he'd had a few drinks), take him far from the maddening crowd, and ask for his daughter's hand in marriage. Maybe it is because I am British and grew up watching the BBC's mini-series of Charles Dickens and the Brontë Sisters that I felt compelled to ask permission. Hopefully, with Jim's blessing, I would propose to Susan during the weekend and then sometime after the excitement from the wedding and reception had died down, announce our engagement.

Question 82: What exactly *is* the Hokey Pokey all about?

I felt a great deal of pressure. I knew this would be the one and only time in my life I would ask this question. Would it really be so bad if I just looked up from across the breakfast table one morning in a disheveled state and, between mouthfuls of Special K, blurted out, "Will you marry me?" Yes, it would. I needed to show her how important she was to me.

Considering each part of the proposal process separately made me more and more anxious about the whole of it. The decisions surrounding the ring alone are enough to bring a grown man to his knees. What style? The setting? Number of carats? I was aware of the guidelines dictating how much one should spend on the ring—twenty percent of one's annual income, or three months of one's take-home pay. But who came up with these guidelines? It seems unlikely that any of the men I know would have suggested them. Maybe it's my cynical nature, but I suspect they were created by jewelry store owners. My distrust aside, it was nevertheless helpful to have some guidelines. My income as an actor in Denver, combined with my income from my small bicycle parts business, meant I was able to quickly calculate that twenty percent of zero is zero and three months of my take-home pay was, astonishingly, also zero. Even though Tom Shane constantly assured me on the local radio that I've got a friend in the diamond business, I suspected he was much better friends with people who had money.

Since a traditional engagement ring seemed unlikely, I focused my energy on picking a spectacular location that would outshine the conspicuous absence of fine jewelry. Anywhere in New York City had to be perfect, plus I already had nailed down the "when."

Having the location and date firmly in place, I didn't feel compelled to plan any further. I had to be careful. Over-planning could ultimately result in crushing the spontaneity of the moment.

Question 86: Does Waldo *know* he's lost?

I tensed. My hands gripped the armrests. The plane landed with a harsh bump followed immediately by the urgent sound of both engines in reverse thrust as the pilot wrestled the 737 to a manageable speed. Our speed continued to reduce, and I relaxed as the friendly voice of the flight attendant floated through the cabin, "Welcome to LaGuardia Airport. Local time is 3:42 p.m."

The hesitant start, then steady rumble of a grubby, overworked sliding door released us from baggage claim into the late afternoon of an August day in New York City. We walked out and hit a wall of humidity. It felt as if on this scorching ninety-eight-degree day I was being forced to don a thick tweed jacket, corduroy pants, a woolly cap, and earmuffs. Perspiration immediately leaked from every pore and turned my light blue shirt into a mood ring. The more sultry my mood, the darker blue it became.

We stood in a sweltering line and waited for a cab. I dreamt of Italian ices, fresh chilled lemonade, and deodorant. A cab drew up and our baggage was loaded into the trunk with the disgruntled, perfunctory efficiency that I've learned is quintessential New York. The cab door shut. We were sealed in, our nostrils challenged to decipher the complicated aroma that heavily hinted of over-zealous evenings in bars ending badly and the many dark blue mood rings that preceded us.

I gave the driver the address. He cheerily said something in a thick accent that I could not understand. I smiled, nodded knowingly, and said thank you. A quick glance at his taxicab driver's permit, proudly displayed behind a cracked Perspex sheet, revealed his name. Vowels outnumbered consonants three to one but shed no light on the origin of his accent. The lackadaisical A/C sputtered ineffectively, and I felt like pounding my hand on the roof of the cab—much, I imagine, like a lobster in a pot.

I braced myself for the ride. Fortunately, our driver was skilled. Disregarding all signs and most white lines, he navigated our little yellow cab into the river of heavy traffic. He had us gliding back and forth, ebbing and flowing, all with the confidence of a man who has exceptional insurance. I relaxed. We were obviously in the hands of a master. I concluded that staring intently out the front windscreen was not constructive. I sat back and enjoyed the ride as I watched a blurred New York City slip silently by the side window, the very city in which I would soon commit myself to love, cherish, and hold until death do us part.

Susan and I carried our bags up a flight of stairs and pushed open the hollow, plywood door of a typical dorm room. Stacy worked at Iona College, and they had kindly allowed the entire Hennessy family to take over part of the dorms for the wedding weekend. This way we could be all together, and what we sacrificed in luxury we more than gained in convenience and affordability. Susan and I settled in and studied the itinerary of organized festivities. Tonight there was to be a cocktail party and light dinner, tomorrow would be the rehearsal dinner, followed the next day by a late afternoon wedding and reception. I decided to ask Jim and Barbara Hennessy for their daughter's hand in marriage after we all returned from the cocktail party, hopefully with a couple of martinis in us. This would give me two days to find the perfect time to pop the question and still announce our engagement after the wedding reception, but before the family departed.

Question 89: If everything that happens there *stays*
there,
will Vegas eventually get full?

Later that night I hovered outside Mr. Hennessy's door, aware that all I had to do was knock. Yet I was unable to do it. The cocktail party (and particularly the cocktails themselves) had definitely elevated my confidence, but the dinner afterward combined with the travel time back to the dorms meant my liquid courage was fast evaporating. *Knock. Just knock. Knock, you poncey bastard.* My hand rose, my fist clenched, and my knuckles tentatively tapped the door. No response. *Perhaps a little too tentative for the human ear to detect. Come on Taylor, knock like a man.* My second attempt solicited a quizzical "Come in." It worked. My knuckles stinging, I entered and instantly realized I might have hovered for too long in the corridor. There on the bed sat Mr. Hennessy wearing nothing but boxer shorts and a T-shirt. Mrs. Hennessy, comfortably settled upon the opposite bed, wore, fortunately, a full complement of clothing.

Had it been any other circumstance, I would have immediately excused myself and scurried out muttering apologies for the intrusion. But now was my moment; I had to push forward. I gently swung the door shut, stepped further into the room and cut to the chase. "Mr. and Mrs. Hennessy, I am in love with Susan and I would like your permission to ask for her hand in marriage." I think I caught them a little off guard. The pause that followed felt like an eternity.

What I hadn't bargained for was an exam. If I had known there was to be a test, I would have studied. I should have also realized Jim had been through this a few times prior and was well-equipped to extract the maximum squirm factor from a future son-in-law. Jim looked directly at me, his face serious, and said, "How do you know you love my daughter?" *Whoa, whoa, heavy first question,* Jim.

Cogs churned as I applied every ounce of my intellect to compose the perfect response. When surprised by an unexpected question, I have trained myself to mutter a phrase or two of inconsequential banter to buy myself time. What came out of my mouth in a hesitant I'm-thinking-way-too-hard-to-hear-what-I'm-actually-saying way was, "Ooh. Ahh … I don't know. Umm. I guess …"

"I don't know" and "I guess" are not answers fathers are looking for when it comes to the lifelong happiness and well-being of their beloved daughters.

The questions kept coming:

How old are you? (I got 100% on that one.)

How old is Susan? (75%)

What is your definition of marriage? *What?*

How do you plan to support my daughter?

Panic swept over me. Finances have never been my strong suit, but they are the number one cause of failed marriages. I had to come up with something good. Mouth dry, palms moist, beads of sweat developing on my forehead, the pressure built as I struggled with the question. I was in danger of losing control. *Keep calm.* I remembered an old speech and debate technique: When flustered, picture your audience in their underwear.

Done.

I battled through the barrage of questions relying heavily on lines such as, "I love Susan," "I love your daughter," and "I love your daughter, Susan." Every now and then I changed it up. "We love each other." "We're in love." "We're in love with each other."

My excessive use of the word "love" achieved my goal. Jim slowly raised himself from the bed, looked at me man-to-man, and said, "You have my permission. Good luck." He smiled and embraced me warmly. His arms wrapped tightly around me, his actions spoke louder than his words. I was welcomed into the Hennessy family.

Question 91: Where *does* John Cougar Mellencamp camp?

I still hadn't pinpointed specifically where in New York or when exactly I was going to pop the question. Now I was down to little over half a day. The morning of the wedding, Susan and I had arranged to meet our friend Steve Lattanzi for breakfast and afterwards we were to link up with Susan's college buddy Andrew Flatt to go to Fire Island. I was confident the perfect moment would arise during the course of the morning.

The steps of the subway station spat us out into the hustle and bustle of the Upper West Side. Seasoned New Yorkers seemed oblivious to the steady drizzle and gray sky. We jockeyed our way to Broadway and 112th. A large pink neon sign proclaiming "Tom's Restaurant" heralded our arrival. I gazed at the sign, along with a dozen other tourists, feeling as if I'd been there a hundred times before with Jerry, George, Elaine, and Kramer. We found Steve seated inside the restaurant which, disappointingly, bore no resemblance to the TV show. We slid into the booth opposite Steve and ordered coffees. *Not here. It's too cheesy. A romantic beach on Fire Island, perhaps — the mist curling off the water's edge ... our eyes meet ... we both know the time has come ...*

Suddenly I noticed the charming, impeccably dressed, and bespectacled figure of Andrew Flatt standing next to our table, his presence a marker that an entire hour had passed. I was jolted back to my mission. We said goodbye to Steve and looked to Andrew for guidance with ferries and timetables as we left the restaurant. He spoke in the confident and succinct manner of a successful executive. "It's an awful day, no point in going to Fire Island." *There goes my plan.* He looked up at the gloomy gray sky and continued, "It's such a horrible day, we should go to the top of the Empire State Building instead. There'll be no line because there sure as hell won't be a view." Susan was enthusiastic about the eccentric idea. I realized I had no say; I was just along for the ride. Besides, all I really wanted was for Andrew to stop saying it's a horribly awful day.

Then it dawned on me: The Empire State Building. Perfect. *An Affair to Remember.* There is no more romantic place in New York to propose than the observation deck of the Empire State Building. I can't say I would have planned it, but we were now heading directly to Proposal Central.

Absorbed in their reminiscing, Susan and Andrew set off at a quick clip towards the subway station. I could procrastinate no longer. I lagged behind to do some rapid planning. I had to find flowers, a card, not to mention extra time to write some well-chosen words. And then, of course, I still needed something to put on her finger. I had to accomplish all of this between 112th and 33rd Streets—and for a large portion of that distance we'd be underground. Susan and Andrew reached the subway station. They looked back and waved, urging me to catch up. I waved back while surveying my surroundings, hoping to find a florist next to a Hallmark store near a jeweler who happened to be giving away diamond rings.

I jogged to the station to join my fellow travelers. I now had to complete my tasks in the short distance between the subway stop and the entrance to the Empire State Building. Things were getting tight. Most event planners take months to pull off a big event. I had three hundred yards. I rode the subway grasping the rail above my head a little tighter than was necessary as I rattled my way towards a proposal.

We surfaced with Andrew leading the charge. He turned right and took off with a New York stride. If he wasn't anticipating a line, why was he in such a bloody hurry? I had magic to create. I glanced around. We were in the heart of the Lower East Side tourist trap. If I were shopping for a Statue of Liberty T-shirt, an I "Heart" NY bumper sticker, or a hooker, I was in the right place. But as for my current needs, the area offered little help. I spotted a shop with a small selection of flowers outside on the sidewalk. I snatched a bouquet of stargazers already wrapped in cellophane and darted into the store to pay. The gentleman behind the counter looked at my purchase and smiled. He said, "Ah, I remember the first stargazer I bought as if it were only yesterday. I was eighteen and in love for the very first time…oh sweet, sweet love. How sweet this thing called love can…" My jaw dropped open. I mouthed, *I don't care.* But there was no stopping him. He started to rewrap the flowers while painfully misquoting passages from Shakespeare and Byron. I tried to tell him there was no need for a bow, but as far as he was concerned a bow was mandatory. He painstakingly applied one. *Stop it! By the time you finish the sodding bow Susan will have married somebody else.* What were the chances? There I was in New York City, famed for its gruff, impersonal, efficient, no-nonsense customer service, and I was prisoner to the city's only floral performance artist.

I ran down the sidewalk. The Empire State Building loomed ahead, its familiar silhouette pointing skyward. Susan and Andrew headed in, barely noticing my absence. Next to the entrance was a postcard shop. I grabbed the card nearest to me. In a single bound I landed at the counter. To my relief, the transaction was conducted in the unfriendly matter-of-fact fashion I hoped for. I passed through the main door of the Empire State Building and scooted up to Andrew and my future wife. Susan looked surprised at the flowers. I casually said they were for her sister. It wasn't until we arrived in front of the cashier and were purchasing our tickets that I realized I had missed something. What could I slip on her finger?

I looked directly at the large blue nametag affixed to the sales lady squished into her tiny ticket booth. With pleading eyes, I asked LaTonya if I could borrow her pen. She looked at me as if I'd asked to borrow three hundred feet of her lower intestines. "If I lend you this, I'll never see it again," she said curtly. I said, "I'll use it right here and hand it back." "You'll hold up the other people," she retorted. "I just need to write six words on this card."

Reluctantly, she slid the pen under the thick glass. I feverishly wrote on one side of the postcard, "Will you marry me?" I then rammed my finger through it. Making a jagged hole in the middle, I wrote two more words— "The Ring"—and an arrow pointing towards the hole. Perfect! I chucked the pen back under the glass at LaTonya.

I arrived just in time to be herded into the elevator with Susan, Andrew, and twenty-two other tourists. The doors closed and we were whisked to the heavens. We spat out onto the observation deck, into the fresh air. It was happening too quickly. All I could think was, *Here we are. This is it.* People milled around as people do when they go somewhere specifically for the view and the view isn't there. A large number of them gazed out over the balcony, into the grey clouds, hoping to suddenly get a glimpse of the city below. One extremely optimistic gentleman invested twenty-five cents in the viewing telescope.

We stood at the edge of the balcony, Susan and Andrew still chatting away. I wondered if there was such a thing as the "perfect" moment or the perfect amount of preparation. Then I realized any moment would be perfect if I wanted it to be. I gingerly lowered to one knee and tapped Susan on the back. She turned around, I cleared my throat, my heart pounded, and I said, "I have something important to ask you."

7
PRIVATE PARTS

TIMES CHANGE.

As a child growing up with two sisters in England, it was common practice for parents to call their children's private body parts by cute little nicknames to avoid, heaven forbid, having to use the proper terms. My family was no exception. I had a willy and was flanked by a couple of veronicas. My friends had a nina, a twinkle, a hoo-hoo, and a dingle. I'd heard of other kids sporting a suzie, a hoo-ha, a nah-nee, and a ding-dong. At school I met a peter, a pee-pee, a wiener, goolies, and girlie-bits. By the time I was ten I'd even heard of a weenis, a tally whacker, lady business, the boys at the ballpark, and a meat n' two veg'.

As if it isn't difficult enough for a young child just starting out in life, it seems unfair that we complicate their early years by introducing artificial names, which just have to be awkwardly unlearned later. Now I have my own children, and it is the norm for us to tell our children that a vagina is in fact called a vagina and a penis, a penis. This simplified things—or so I thought.

One hot summer day as my daughter Maitland and son Alastair were roughhousing at the local neighborhood playground Maitland accidentally kicked Alastair between the legs. He crumpled to the ground, hands clasping the injured parties, experiencing that intense pain that can only be experienced if you possess testicles and are unlucky enough to have them kicked. Your throat is instantly dry, your head dizzy with a hint of nausea. An agonizing cramping ache crawls deep into the pit of your stomach. Shear, steady, unyielding pain that stubbornly refuses to pass lingers for what seems like eternity, as if to scold you for putting the crown jewels in harm's way.

Alastair rolled over, his face contorted. He looked up at his apologetic and confused sister. His lips parted as he uttered a single sentence, "Maitland," he said in a high-pitched, pained voice, "you kicked me right in my ball-gina!"

8
FOR THE LOVE OF ART

THERE IT STANDS: true, upright, and strong. Impervious to the elements. Blond in color, broad in stature, built to last, a monument to good craftsmanship. My fence. How could I possibly have known that this monument was destined to become a memorial?

I have been working on my house and yard for the last fourteen years. One day I will wake up and realize there is nothing left to do. Then I will sell it. Being utterly untrained and unskilled in both construction and landscaping, I have been forced to adopt two distinct tactics. First, I recruit a friend who has knowledge and skill applicable to the task at hand. The second tactic is to jump in wildly. My goal is to reach the point of no return within the first hour of the project. I then have no choice but to continue, however uncomfortable or inconvenient I have made my life.

The master plan for the yard proved to be a classic case study. My friend, Kris Larson, a proud recipient of a master's degree in Landscape Architecture, eagerly measured, designed, and drew up plans. Over several beers, we fine-tuned the plans until they were perfect. We called Hoppe, another good friend heavily armed with a Landscape Architecture degree, who also possessed the enviable skill of Bobcat operator. Luckily, he was happy to help, too.

The only day we couldn't start was the first Saturday in May. The first Saturday in May is reserved for the running of the Kentucky Derby. My wife is from Louisville, and every year we have a large Kentucky Derby party. So in typical Matthew-style, it was no surprise to find Kris, Hoppe, and me in the garden with a rented Bobcat on the first Friday in May—twenty-four hours before one hundred elegantly dressed and elaborately topped Derby guests were to arrive. Within an hour, Hoppe had skillfully pulled down old fences, dug up tons of concrete driveway, and started to level the ground according to specifications detailed in the Master Plan.

By the end of the day most of the concrete had been removed, the main level set, and the excess soil strategically placed in mounds. Like most projects, the first day is always the most productive. Demolition is not only satisfying, but also quick. The one drawback of demolition is that once completed, there is no choice but to engage in the slow and painstaking task of reconstruction.

The only difference between a garden and a worksite is looseness. A garden is compacted. It doesn't move easily, and it's often contained by stonework or topped with a surface such as grass to ensure that when you wake up in the morning it is still in the same place it was the night before. Once you move soil around, it becomes loose and acquires a mind of its own. And until it settles or is retained, it can surprise you with its ability to rearrange itself. It is at this point one becomes aware of the Equation of Mud, which is:

$$\frac{Soil + Water}{Looseness} = Mud$$

We had moved every molecule of soil in my backyard. Add to this the removal of any retention, stir in a steady May drizzle, and voilà, we had unwittingly created the world's largest experiment in mud formation. It was just one gigantic, vaguely terraced mud-fest. Needless to say, the going for the following day's Derby party was likely to be heavy.

After a sleepless night, I awoke that Saturday and was greeted by sunshine. One of the great benefits of living in Denver is being a mile above sea level. When the sun does come out, things dry remarkably quickly. Thankfully, my mud garden had not left the starting gate and appeared to be setting up nicely. I purchased a couple of hay bales, which I thought created a clever horserace-related theme. I broke them up and spread a three-inch layer over everything. Kris kindly returned and quickly built temporary steps (which, incidentally, remain to this day) constructed with Colorado red stone to allow the guests to move from the lower level of mud to the higher level of mud. Pleased with his work, Kris rushed home, washed up, and returned accompanied by his family to enjoy what proved to be a very successful Derby party. Then he moved to Minnesota.

With the master architect, motivator, and skilled craftsman gone, I spent the next two-and-a-half years marveling at friends who taught me how to: build a one-hundred-forty-eight-foot dry stone wall; lay a four-hundred-eighty-square-foot stone patio, complete with pergola; install a seven-zone, sixty-three head sprinkler system; and plant numerous trees, shrubs, and flowers.

Eventually, thanks to my talented friends, the garden took shape. The only major project that remained was the rear fence and gate. It was now spring once again. The ski season had ended, which meant my dear friend Art might be available for a little project. Art and I had become the closest of friends when I lived in Crested Butte, Colorado. We were inseparable for the five years I spent there and had done a lot of skiing, biking, working, and general misbehaving together.

After I moved away, Art started doing construction and eventually formed his own company, building beautiful Crested Butte homes. A nice turn of events for me, since my little fence would be something Art could do in his sleep. As luck would have it, he was going to make a trip to Denver the following week to pick up some tile for a job. So, we planned to do the fence the same day.

The main difference between me and people who do construction for a living is the amount of time I spend looking at a project. For some reason, I can't just start. There is a whole process I go through to examine every possible scenario, both good and bad, while psyching myself up.

The measuring process alone can take me two days. The measurement is clearly eight feet, two-and-a-quarter inches, *but how could it be?* I measure again. Eight feet, two-and-a-quarter inches. *Wow, what are the chances of that? I'd better check it again.* So, I re-measure and only after recording a measurement of eight feet, two-and-a-quarter inches will I reluctantly accept the fact that it might actually be a little over eight feet. *But how much over?* I'll mark off eight feet and spend more time working to establish the exact amount. Eventually, I will arrive at a figure of two-and-a-quarter inches. By now it's time for a break, at the end of which I will have most likely forgotten the original measurement and need to start again.

A giant, black pickup truck barreled up outside my house, heralding the arrival of skilled labor. My morning inspection of the snow-dusted jobsite concerned me. The damp, overcast Colorado day almost certainly meant it was too cold to work with concrete. As wonderful as it would be to see Art, a piece of me lamented the fact that his expertise might slip though my fingers.

He leapt out of the truck and bounded up the temporary steps of the garden. Art is an unusual mix of Viking and Golden Retriever puppy. He is deceptively broad and tall, a fact cleverly disguised by his perfect body proportion and only evident when he dwarfs me in a bear hug. He grew up on a small farm in Minnesota. His fair skin, ample strawberry blonde hair, and immense strength confirm his northern heritage. His muscles are not clearly defined like someone who spends hours lifting weights in a gym. They are more rounded, one muscle running smoothly into another. Art is coated with muscle and deep inside him is the heart of a lion. His thick hair lives in perpetual defiance of all the combs and brushes of the world. A visor pushes this lawless mass up and out of the top, allowing it to randomly point in every direction.

As much as Art's physical traits point firmly towards his Scandinavian heritage, his behavior and character are those of a puppy. He always arrives with a level of eager anticipation seldom seen among humans, almost as if he expects you to throw something for him to fetch. His boundless energy allows him to play forever, whether it be in snow, on a bike, or at work. If Art had lived during the heyday of the Vikings, their legacy might well have been very different, with a reputation of giant men who licked entire villages to death.

Within a minute of Art's arrival, he was at work. The freezing weather seemed to be of no concern. Whether it was because it was of no concern, or because he was building my fence, and not his fence, I didn't know. He took the tape from my hand and used it with the confidence of a man who has never been lied to by a tape measure. Within three minutes, he completed the measurements and had written a materials list right down to the seventy-eight pickets that would be required. Moments later we were in the truck heading for Home Depot, my face beaming with a foolish ear-to-ear grin.

I have always had a love/hate relationship with Home Depot. If it wasn't for the mobile bratwurst cart out front, it would be hard for me to enter the parking lot and not feel overwhelmed by the task at hand. The fact that there is always more than one item or material that can be used for a particular job means the majority of my time in the store is spent jockeying for the attention of a dubiously qualified "specialist" clad in an orange apron. To give the staff credit, they are nearly always friendly and try to be helpful. The problem is I can never fully grasp their rushed instructions. I feel guilty and pressured to hurry so as not to dominate the time of a person who is in such demand; a person constantly trailed by anxious customers, many of them clutching defunct pieces of hardware. (I think therapists around the world might consider recommending that anybody who is depressed, lonely, or feeling unappreciated should apply for a job at Home Depot.)

Today was different. Art and I moved skillfully through the gigantic aisles and filled the cart efficiently. We checked out, loaded up, and rented an auger to bore the post holes. The renting of the auger went smoothly, though I did struggle to purge from my mind the disaster that had occurred the last time I rented one for the construction of our backyard pergola. I bored the first hole straight through my main sewer line, which backed things up a bit.

I could sense that with Art here, there would be no mishaps. We were back at the jobsite in less than forty-five minutes. The snow cleared, the auger started, holes were bored, and in no time I was returning the auger. Back at the site, the fence posts were bolted to the house and the garage. The remaining ones were placed in holes with dry concrete mix poured around them. We hosed the holes down and mixed the concrete, then set the posts level and true. I would have now left them to set for a day or two, but not Art. As soon as they were in place, he was measuring and cutting the rails to run between the posts. Up they went, screwed directly into the yet-to-set posts. "Let's go collect my tile while these set up a bit," Art said, already halfway to the truck.

Forty minutes later, the tile was being forklifted into the truck bed and we headed home. Art was not in a resting mood. He surveyed his surroundings and said, more to himself than to me, "Build the gate, hang the pickets, affix hardware, and we're done." And that's what happened. By four o'clock in the afternoon, Art was setting a few braces to ensure the whole fence would set up true. We were finished.

Art decided to try and beat rush hour. We would be seeing each other in a few weeks for a bike trip we'd planned, so anything we hadn't caught up on during the day we'd be able to do at our leisure on the ride. Away he drove, off into the chilly early evening, leaving in his wake a fine-looking fence and a highly impressed and thankful friend.

On a glorious late spring day a couple of weeks later, I was sitting on my patio, enjoying a mid-morning cup of coffee, looking out across the garden with the fence behind me. I decided to call Art since we needed to nail down the last few details of the following week's bike trip. I punched in an "A," then an "R," and "Art Thilquist's

Cell" popped up on the display. I pushed the green button and the phone kindly told me it was dialing.

It is from this point on that, if I were simply making up a story, I would alter it. But with a real-life story, the details cannot be changed. There is nothing I can do but tell the truth. The beauty of real life is just that: it's real.

Art didn't answer the phone. Kate, Art's longtime girlfriend, did. "Matthew?" she said. Her tone carried an unmistakable mixture of panic, fear, and dread. I could sense the dryness in her mouth. I instantly knew that what she was about to say I did not want to hear. "Art's had a bad fall on the building site. A really bad fall. He's unconscious and is being flown to Grand Junction. I'm leaving right now to drive there. I'll call you when I know more." By the end of this short exchange, her voice was breaking. I was so shocked I could offer little in response. She hung up.

I sat in stunned silence. My mind raced as I tried to make sense of the limited information I'd been given. I kept reassuring myself that Art had the strength of three men and if anyone could fight this and come out on top, Art was the man. But I was crippled by the lack of information, and as always, when not given the full picture, I started filling in the gaps. And however hard I tried to fill them in positively, a darker picture emerged.

Having lived in Crested Butte, I'd seen the comings and goings of the Flight for Life helicopter, yet if I was asked what were the results from each flight I would have to confess I had no idea. What percentage lived or died? It didn't help that I am constantly reminded of this since my house is in the direct flight path for St. Anthony

Hospital on the south side of Sloan Lake. Every few days an orange and yellow helicopter flies low over my home, its rotors spin with an urgency that declares the importance of its mission. I always gaze skyward, send up a prayer, and wonder where it's going and whose life has just been turned inside-out in an uncontrollable second. Now it was my life. My best friend was in a helicopter fighting for his life, flying somewhere on the other side of the mountains. And all I could do was pray and wait.

I went back into the house and refilled my coffee. I slumped down on a chair, but the confines of the walls and ceiling quickly closed in on me. I felt pressure building inside my numbed, confused, and frightened head. I jumped up and headed outside to get some fresh air. As I walked out the back door and onto the patio, I turned left towards the table and chairs, and there it stood.

True, upright, and strong. Impervious to the elements. Blond in color, broad in stature, built to last, a monument to good craftsmanship.

My fence.

9
AND AS WE WIND ON DOWN THE ROAD

I HEARD BEN HAUGH, landlord of the Shore Inn, bark his famously gruff and completely unintelligible call for last orders, signaling an epic Saturday night drinking session drawing to a close. Twenty minutes later and another pint better, my mate, Steve Nyland, and I spilled out into the car park at 11:00 p.m. I know by American standards the night was still young. Many Americans, especially skillful drinkers, don't even start the evening's intake and carousing until 11:00 p.m. Yet, there we stood in East Wittering, two twenty-two-year-olds in a chilly car park, our drinking options terminated by the good ol' British licensing laws. Of course, we wanted to prolong the evening and be legally permitted to continue drinking.

Yes, there are two paths you can go by ...

The first path is to head to the local Tandoori restaurant. Indian restaurants are extremely popular throughout Britain. And most offer decent food at reasonable prices. What separates them from all the other restaurants is their proprietor's work ethic. Their hours of operation far exceed those of most other establishments, which by 11:00 p.m. have long since closed, their owners all comfortably tucked up in bed. Most Indian restaurants have a liquor license that allows them to serve their patrons alcohol as long as they are dining.

Needless to say, ten minutes after the pubs close, there's usually a line of wobbly individuals trudging towards the local Tandoori restaurant, all in search of an unnecessary plate of curry and an even more unnecessary mug of beer. This late night pilgrimage is obviously a bit of a cash cow for the restaurant, but this extra money comes at a hefty price. The unfortunate owners have to put up with the abhorrent behavior of the late-night British drunk. My dislike of curry stems from one of these experiences.

One morning, walking to work in the steady English drizzle following a boisterous night out, seeking warmth, I plunged my hand deep into the pocket of my heavy overcoat. My hand met with the slightly gelatinous, lukewarm chicken vindaloo that my friends had poured into my pocket when I dozed off at the table the previous evening. This unsavory culinary memory ruined my enjoyment of curry forever.

The second path to after-hours drinking leads you down the dangerous road to the local nightclub scene. The word nightclub can be misleading, since Studio 54 was a nightclub, but so apparently is The Pond Barn in Bracklesham Bay. The word nightclub is the only similarity between the two. The problem with the British nightclub scene is that, unlike the local Indian restaurant, they are rarely within stumbling distance. This means a cab ride or finding an idiot who thinks he's sober enough to drive. While Steve and I wandered around outside the pub pondering our two options, we overheard the distinctive voice of an idiot. Our decision was made. We wedged into the backseat of Simon Groom's parents' white Ford Escort, and with a squeal of rubber, peeled out of the Shore Inn parking lot and off into the night.

Simon and his friend John, who occupied the front passenger seat, were not guys with whom we hung around. They were different from us. First off, they were bigger and stronger due to the various forms of manual labor they regularly performed. Secondly, their sense of humor was coarser and less complicated. They did occasionally laugh, but unlike us, they would never giggle. For them humor only occurred in the early part of the evening and usually at somebody else's expense. By the end of the night, they took offense easily and were incapable of offering apologies. This led to many evenings ending in blows or a considerable amount of property damage. There was little lightness in their conversation. Words like *hijinks* and *revelry* were absent from their vocabulary. I often thought these guys were capable of doing things I would never dare or even want to do. The fact that Steve and I were now sitting in a car completely at the mercy of these two hoodlums is evidence that I rarely made wise decisions with six pints inside me.

To compound matters, we weren't headed a couple of miles down the road to The Pond Barn; we were headed to Visions in Bognor Regis. Any town with the name Bognor is off to a poor start. Just saying the word Bognor conjures up the image of an unpleasant smelling marsh that is too large to walk around. It's just a shitty name for a popular seaside resort. Visions Night Club had a sinister reputation for violence. Everyone knew that the local lads would cause serious trouble at the drop of a hat. I found solace in the fact that I was wearing running shoes. I was confident that some nimble movement would be required at some point during the wee hours of the morning.

Bognor is about ten miles to the east of East Wittering, which is home to The Shore Inn. Amazingly, even in his impaired state, Simon wisely opted to take the back lanes to avoid as many major roads as possible. However, he still drove like a madman who was possessed by the ghost of a madman, who had lived as a racecar driver who was possibly mad. And in that fashion, he thrashed the Ford Escort within an inch of its life.

Steve and I were thrown back and forth and side to side as Simon squealed and jerked from one turn to the next. The high hedgerows and narrow lanes made it feel like we were on a terrifying fairground ride being operated by a drunk carny with only two teeth. Again and again, as we approached a corner, Simon slammed on the brakes at the very last second and then aggressively accelerated around the bend. On blind corners, he turned off his headlights completely to confirm that no headlights were coming the other way; then he flipped his lights back on and flew around the corner, using every inch of the road.

My wide open eyes were glued to the twisting lane ahead of me. Every now and then I glanced out the side window, but only for a moment. Watching the blurred hedgerows zip by only inches away from our car was more disturbing than looking ahead. I had been on my fair share of crazy car rides, but this was taking things to another level. I feared for my life on every turn. I couldn't even muster the words to suggest that he slow down. I had completely forgotten the fact that we were headed to Bognor Regis and destined for a certain beating that now seemed like something to look forward to.

We were fast approaching the village of Sidlesham, with Mario Andretti showing no signs of slowing down, when I noticed something ahead of us. It looked like a car with no lights on, parked up on the verge with a person standing in the road. I didn't think Simon had seen them because there was no reduction in our speed. As we zoomed closer, the scene became crystal clear: a police speed trap. Out to catch idiots. I let out a sigh. "Oh well," I thought to myself, "Simon is busted." The policeman in the road turned on a red flashlight and waved it up and down towards us as we approached. He must have already clocked the insane speed at which we were traveling and now it was just a matter of pulling us over, administering the Breathalyzer, and completing the paperwork. In a way, I was secretly relieved; Simon's insane driving had shaken me more than I cared to admit. Our journey coming to an end was okay by me.

I glanced for the first time at Steve sitting next to me, and he too seemed relieved the adventure was drawing to a close. Simon at last eased up on the gas, now aware of the grim circumstances. The police officer slowly and rhythmically waved the red light at the side of the road. I could see him clearly in our headlights; young and lean in his crisp new uniform, a reflective armband and a policeman hat with a black-and-white checkered band around it. I saw the police car parked to the side with another police officer sitting in the driver's seat, ready to start the process of stripping Simon of his right to ever again operate a motor vehicle. *This is about to become a long night,* I thought to myself as we drew within twenty-five feet.

One of the benefits of spending time with people who are unlike me is that they help me gain a different perspective. People have always fascinated me, and I can always learn from them. Some of these lessons I will hold dear; others I choose to let go of. But if I listen and watch, I am invariably richer for the experience, even if the experience is not something I expect.

I don't know what surprised me the most—the sudden acceleration of our vehicle or the size of the young policeman's eyes when we did so. We covered the last twenty-five feet in a blink. The policeman's flashlight accelerated along with us. By the time we flew past him, his arm was swinging up and down like the wing of a hummingbird. I turned and looked helplessly out the side window as we flew past him. Our two pairs of wide, startled eyes met for a split-second. Both of us were clearly stunned at the break in routine. I spun around and looked out the back window. The young policeman stared back at me in disbelief as we sped away. The other more experienced officer wasn't so shocked. He had already fired up the police car. Lights came on, followed by the siren, which screamed at us as we rounded a corner on two wheels.

WHAT THE HELL! I was now involved in a full-fledged police chase. With the certainty of the loss of his license, jail, and the possibility of a firing squad looming, Simon was spurred on to drive more recklessly than before. Steve and I rolled around in the backseat, trying to brace ourselves both physically and mentally. Every now and then I glimpsed the flashing lights behind us. We'd make a quick turn and they would disappear. We had a thirty- to forty-five-second advantage over our pursuer. That's pretty impressive for a Ford Escort. We screeched around corners, brushing hedgerows and clipping curbs. I clung to the door handle and wedged myself into the corner, bracing my foot on the back of the driver's seat, slightly twisted so I could look out the back window. Every time the road straightened, the police car swung back into view, its colored lights flashing angrily at us.

I was sure our capture was inevitable even before reinforcements arrived, which I assumed were efficiently on the way. This much excitement in Sidlesham didn't happen every night and there was no way the other local Bobbies would want to miss out.

The next time I saw our pursuers they were definitely gaining on us. Words started to pop into my head: Accomplice, Accessory, Aiding and Abetting. These were all words I was familiar with, but I realized I didn't know their exact definitions. I wanted details. What makes an accomplice an accomplice? What's the definition of an accessory to a crime? Is it intent? Proximity? How does one abet? Steve and I were merely in the backseat of a car at the wrong time; surely we couldn't be held accountable for the actions of the driver. Or could we? If we were culpable, where would the line be drawn? What if Simon had been towing a U-Haul trailer and Steve and I were in there? Would we still be accomplices even if we couldn't see what was happening and were connected to Simon's Ford Escort by only a tow-bar? I came to the conclusion that most likely these phrases and words are kept purposely vague so as to allow the police to apply the law to anyone who just happens to be in the general vicinity of a crime, or in our case, the backseat of a crime.

A particularly vicious jerk to the left was immediately followed by Simon's first comment. "Get ready! We're going to exit!" What the hell did that mean? I was fast learning that when a crime is in process, details tend to be sketchy at best. With the police car out of view, we violently veered off the road and up onto the parking lot of the Sidlesham gas station. We screeched to a halt next to a line of cars for sale. *Clever move*, I thought. It would take longer for the police to find the car here than if we just abandoned it on the side of the road and ran. I thought to myself, *Simon has done this before.*

All four doors of our car swung open simultaneously and we piled out. Simon led the charge. I had a split second to decide. Stay. Be arrested. And be quoted in the *Chichester Observer* saying, "Society is to blame," or run with the thugs. My many questions unanswered, my choice was clear: run like the wind.

Off we went following Simon into a ditch down the side of a mechanic's shop. Halfway along the side of the building, Simon came to an abrupt halt. We all froze. There we stood, up to our waists in brambles.

Most ditches in southern England are infested with brambles. They quickly take over, weaving their thick, matted tendrils every which way into a tangled mess. Their hard and unforgiving thorns stand in sharp contrast to the sweet blackberries they offer up once a year. We were pinned. Each of us had a minimum of eight thorns stabbing at us from our waists down. The brambles got thicker and taller ahead of us. Since we seemed to have thrown our pursuers off our trail, we figured we had a moment to rethink our current prickly strategy. The moment evaporated with the dramatic arrival of the police car. It slid in sideways, lights blazing, doors opening before it even came to a complete standstill, smoke shooting from the tires. It looked just like a TV cop show.

If we had needed a little encouragement to move on, this was just the ticket. Off we sprinted, deep into the thick, high brambles. We were oblivious of the thorns tearing at our clothes and flesh, which left us ripped and bloodied. We pushed on towards the end of the building. Simon turned and threw himself into another ditch. He popped up, wrestled out of the desperate grip of the remaining brambles, and scrambled into the field. We all followed suit. Crouched down in the field, we ran, hugging the twists and turns of the hedgerow.

The brambles gave us some separation from the police. We found an extra thick hedge and stopped for a moment to assess. Three additional police cars rushed on to the scene. It appeared that they had taken personally Simon's decision not to stop at their speed trap and were now a little miffed. Instead of Chase, we were now engaged in a high-stakes game of Hide and Seek. At this point, we were well into farmland, which, in England, consists of large fields delineated by hedges. Most of the fields around us were corn, which had been harvested a few weeks earlier, leaving six-inch stubble. The other nearby fields were grass for grazing. Neither offered any options for cover.

The police were now driving along the lanes that twisted between many of the fields and used their powerful searchlights to scour the hedgerows. It reminded me of a scene from *The Great Escape*, with searchlights sweeping across open land hoping to pin down Steve McQueen.

Crouching in the darkness, torn and bloodied, it dawned on me that my actions to this point would most likely make me an accomplice, an accessory, and probably an abettor. I definitely did not want to be caught. I was sure the evening would be more enjoyable if I got away. My companions wanted to stay in the hedgerows, which certainly gave an impression of safety, but I considered that idea to be suicide. Given the number of police and the amount of hedgerow, it was just a matter of time before we would be found. Plus, the hedgerow would be precisely where they would focus their search first. We needed to prolong their search as long as possible with the hope that they might eventually lose interest and call it off.

My plan was to pick a large field with six-inch corn stubble, crawl out near the middle, and lie perfectly flat. My rationale was that even if a spotlight from the edge of the field crossed over us, it was unlikely we'd be noticed. They would have to start walking the fields in a crisscross search pattern and realistically would have to get within twenty feet to find us.

With the police sweep heading towards us, my plan was accepted. We exchanged some clothing to eliminate all white items, smeared our faces and hands with mud, and began to crawl commando-style on our bellies. We slowly slithered out into the open towards the center of the corn field. I felt exposed leaving the sanctuary of the hedgerows and expected a bright light to hit me at any time, followed by the excited sounds of the capture, but it didn't happen. We kept crawling. It took about ten minutes to get to the middle, where we stopped and let the waiting begin.

Steve and I positioned our heads close to each other so we could whisper strategies while we waited out the cops. Barely raising our heads, we watched the activity around us: cars and lights, muffled commands. Every now and then, when there was a marked increase in activity, it appeared they might have seen us. Once in a while, a searchlight would flash across the corn stubble. One time it washed right over us but then moved on. The police never did search in the fields.

After about forty-five minutes, two police cars left. The third followed them a half-hour later. One last car lingered, driving around and around, stubbornly refusing to let its prey escape. I was sure it was the original car whose occupants would have to endure the endless ribbing of the other officers about the ones that got away.

An hour-and-a-half later, the lights from the final car disappeared down the lane into the distance. We waited an extra half-hour. Simon and John wanted to go back to the car to see if it was still there and drivable. Steve and I said that if it was okay with them, we'd make our own way home. Simon and John started their crawl back to the hedgerow. Steve and I waited a while longer and then crawled in exactly the opposite direction. Our bodies were stiff and sore as they began to respond to the command to move for the first time in nearly three hours, but it also felt wonderful knowing that with every movement the distance between us and them grew.

Upon arrival at the edge of the field, we got up, checked to see that the coast was clear, crossed the hedgerow into the road, and once again thankful for our running shoes, jogged the five miles home. Every time we saw the headlights of a car approaching, we hurriedly jumped into a hedge to hide. While crouched in the relative safety of our rustic refuge, we sang quietly ... and giggled.

If there's a bustle in your hedgerow
Don't be alarmed now,
It's just Steve and Matthew hiding.
Ooh, it makes me wonder.

10
SURPRISE PARTY

IN 2005, THE NEARBY Denver Center Theatre Company put up a show called *Jesus Hates Me*. Personally, I don't think He does. But it would take the beautiful childlike innocence of my six-year-old son to conjure up a plan that just might piss Jesus off.

Alastair's birthday is in August, so it was with much surprise when on a snowy day in March he looked up at me and boldly announced, "I know what type of birthday party I want."

"Wonderful," I said imagining nine pint-sized Spidermen running around the house. "What kind of party do you want, Ali?"

He proudly proclaimed, "A Jesus Party!"

I have to confess my immediate concern—my inability to get a matching tablecloth, paper plates, cups, and napkins from Target. But I had other reservations too. The invitations would now have to be homemade. And it was hard not to imagine the impact when the invitation was opened by children and their parents:

> Come celebrate Alastair's 7th Birthday
> At his Jesus Party
> (Apostle apparel optional)

Needless to say, Alastair's choice of party theme was a surprise to me. Yet, it should not have been. After all, as a family we are regular churchgoers. He's always attended Sunday school. He's been baptized, confirmed, and received first communion. He is an inquisitive boy who loves to absorb information and figure things out. So it was a natural progression to place Jesus at the right hand of God and perhaps to the left hand of Batman, Spiderman, and the Incredible Hulk. In his eyes, they are all superheroes together. And thus, all great fodder for a damn good party. He just had to pick one.

My son's high-pitched voice brought me back to the moment. It became obvious he had given much consideration to the actual planning of his Jesus party.

"Yeah, Dad," he said enthusiastically, "because I think it will be really cool to have a Jesus piñata."

I am a big believer in boundaries. I believe establishing boundaries is hugely important in virtually all aspects of life. I also believe that once a boundary has been established, one of the main reasons for its existence is to push it. I always encourage exploration to discover the endless possibilities that lie just outside the norms. However, pushing is one thing, crossing is another. So once you cross the boundary and start fishing in the murky waters of the taboo, where does the next boundary appear? Or once the line is crossed, do you now exist in a vast boundary-less wasteland where anything goes? I believe that even in this wasteland of moral lawlessness, there is a boundary. And that boundary is a Jesus piñata.

But I have to confess, it does create a very vivid image. The piñata hanging from a tree gently swaying in the light breeze. I see His soft familiar image—long hair, flowing gown, sandals, hands to either side held out slightly from the body in that "all are welcome" way. Below Him, a gang of nine sugar-starved, seven-year-old boys armed with sticks ready to smash Him to bits. It is most likely at this moment that the neighbors would wander down the street and look over the fence. They would offer neighborly smiles and waves as they were drawn back to fond memories of their children's birthday parties. Suddenly, they would stop dead in their tracks, frozen in horror as they noticed the gently swaying piñata. Their mouths would gape while their faces struggled to select the appropriate emotion. Eventually they would settle on a mixture of disgust, contempt, and anger, all smeared with a liberal serving of disbelief.

Alastair tugged at my arm. This time there was a growing excitement in his delivery. He sensed that his choice of birthday party was making quite an impact upon his father. Now, to secure the party of his dreams, he just needed to drive home the sales pitch. It was time to close the deal.

"Hey, Dad, we could also play Pin the Jesus on the Cross!"

It is rare for me to be rendered speechless. This was one of those rare moments. My mouth still moved, silently, opening and closing rhythmically, much like a goldfish. *Is this really happening? If it is, how the hell am I going to get out of this mess? Does he understand the potential flaw in a pin-on game that requires three contact points? Where's my wife? How much does relocation cost? Do they still stone people?* And, of course, *What would Jesus do?*

All these thoughts raced through my mind as an overly-cute, eagerly-awaiting six-year-old gazed up at me with an I-aim-to-please smile on his face.

Now was the time to assert my authority. I would be firm. Crush this idea before it ballooned into a national media shit storm.

"Alastair," I stated firmly, "go ask your mother."

11
LOW SPEED ROBBERY

ON MY LIST OF GREAT American cities, Chicago is right up there at the top. I have visited the Windy City on several occasions, and I am always impressed by how proud Chicagoans are of their city and how hard they work to make my stay as enjoyable and memorable as possible.

I have an unproven theory that the harsher the climatic conditions in an area, the friendlier the locals tend to be. Let's, for a moment, explore my reasoning using Chicago as an example. The insufferable heat and humidity of the summer combined with the arctic conditions and crippling wind chill of the winter months create a formidable common foe. An enemy without prejudice. Weather cares not for race, religion, social or economic standing, age or sexual preference. He wreaks his unpleasant havoc relentlessly upon all, showing neither weakness nor mercy.

This brutal, undiscriminating assault levels life's playing field. The multi-million dollar power broker is affected the same as the hotdog vendor. All are drawn together on equal footing. It is "us" (the people of Chicago) versus "them" (the weather), which builds a true sense of community. We are all in this together, for good or for worse, so we may as well make it for the good.

It was a horribly hot and humid Chicago summer day. My friend Andrew and I had spent the day exploring the Brookfield Zoo. We enjoyed the zoo even though the heat had rendered most of the animals immobile. They just lay around looking at us with questioning eyes, as if to say, "Why can't we take off our fur coats?"

Since we were visiting Chicago for only a few days and staying with a friend, we hadn't rented a car. We depended on public transportation for our sightseeing. We left the zoo on foot and walked to a nearby neighborhood bar, where we hydrated ourselves for a while under the pretense of planning our bus route back to our friend's house in Oakbrook.

There must have been more planning required than I initially realized, since we were still planning several hours later. At last, fully-planned, we left the bar and headed for the bus stop. We had established that our return journey would require exactly one transfer. The fact that it took us three hours to work this out is a testament to the fine brewers of America.

Soon we were aboard, hobnobbing with our fellow Chicagoan bus travelers. Everything ran smoothly and in no time we arrived at the bus stop at which we were to transfer. We alighted and were a little surprised to find out we'd gotten off in Poland. Every business as far as the eye could see was Polish. Most signage was in Polish, everybody looked Polish, even the bus driver looked considerably more Polish than when we had boarded fifteen minutes earlier. The only recognizable business was a nearby bar. Of course it was a Polish bar, but it is amazing how any drinking establishment in any country has a certain familiarity to it when you are English.

Since everything was running so smoothly and we had twenty minutes before our transfer, we felt it would be silly not to spend some time enjoying Poland. We headed towards the familiar and a moment later opened the door to a fine Polish bar whose name had six vowels and a backwards "k." Two Polish bar stools beckoned us, and we settled in between two Polish gentlemen, with a large Polish bartender in front of us.

The room was long and narrow with high ceilings. The bar ran down the entire length of the left-hand side. A row of stools stood in solidarity, prepared to uphold the working class clientele. Booths nestled privately on the opposite wall. The room would have been quite ordinary except for one unmistakable feature—everything in the bar was red.

Not just red but a dark rich red. The floor was red, the walls were red, the ceiling was red, and everything that touched them was red. It was like sitting in a gigantic mouth. It took a minute for our eyes to become accustomed to the complete redness before we could start focusing on our immediate surroundings and fellow patrons.

To one side of us was a tough-looking, stocky, middle-aged Pole who rested heavily on the bar as if he were a load-bearing customer. With alarming regularity, his broad forearm, with a Popeye-sized fist clasping a thick-walled beer mug, rose mindlessly to a blank face, and an inch of liquid then disappeared. The motion seemed almost robotic, and if the man gleaned any pleasure from the repetition he kept it a secret.

On our other flank was a much older member of the Polish community. He also leaned upon the bar, but more from necessity. If the bar were suddenly removed, the old gentleman would collapse into a small Polish pile and it would take an army of Red Cross volunteers to extract his fragile frame from the heap of worn clothing.

He was a small man who continued to shrink before my eyes. His gaunt, wrinkled, weathered face and grey smoke-streaked hair marked a long, hard fight for survival in a foreign country. His sharp, alert eyes proved his tenacity. His clothing was shiny in places where it continually rubbed against his bones. In front of him on the bar rested his small glass of cheap, warm beer. It inched down ever so slowly from an occasional sip.

The bartender stood in front of us. Take a stereotypical, tough working-class bartender, add some Polish to that image, and that's who was standing before us. He said nothing, but his presence seemed to demand a drink order. We obliged and two cold bottles of beer soon arrived, at which point Andrew handed him a twenty-dollar bill.

I settled on my barstool, took a sip of my beer, and became conscious for the first time that everyone in the bar was observing Andrew and me just as hard as I had been studying them. There was a general hush throughout the bar, similar to a saloon in an old western movie the moment after the outlaw walks in.

They weren't hostile, but it created a curiously uncomfortable sensation. I felt guilty even though I knew we hadn't done anything. It didn't take long for my insecure mind to begin playing tricks on me. Perhaps we had done something wrong. I then envisaged what horrible price we were about to pay for our imaginary transgressions.

Ignoring the stares, Andrew and I returned to our bus schedule. During our conversation, Andrew realized he hadn't received any change from the twenty. He glanced at the bar to check if the bartender had placed it there. There was nothing.

So Andrew turned to the bartender and quite casually asked, "Hey Mate, did you give me back my change for the two drinks?" The bartender responded immediately in an aggressive tone, "I put yer change on the bar when I gave yuh the drinks," he growled.

Andrew made a gesture towards the bar to show the bartender that there wasn't a dime anywhere on the bar, let alone the fourteen dollars that was owed to us. At this point, the bartender opted for a physical exchange rather than a verbal one.

He employed a gesture I'd never seen before. He held up both his hands about chest high with his palms towards us. His head tilted to one side. He then moved his palms slightly towards us. His facial expression for the duration of this unusual maneuver was one of slightly pursed lips, flared nostrils, and cold, unblinking eyes. All the while he expressed an edge of controlled anger.

The gesture did the trick. Even though we had no idea what it meant, Andrew and I decided not to continue the conversation with the bartender, but to explore other possibilities for the disappearance of our change. We didn't have to explore very far.

During our encounter with the bartender, neither Andrew nor I had noticed the departure of the fragile gentleman who had been sitting next to us. Now, the last thing we wanted to do was falsely accuse the old man of stealing our change, but there appeared to be some evidence, albeit circumstantial, pointing in his direction.

If the bartender did in fact put the change on the bar, which we both felt was likely, then only one person really could have had the chance to nick it. Plus, the elderly gentleman looked like he lived in this bar, and yet for some strange reason, at 8:30 on a Saturday night, he just took off. Most incriminatingly, he also left a half-full glass of beer.

This was not the sort of man who would ever leave beer. I would bet all our missing change that if he suffered a heart attack while sitting at the bar, he would insist on finishing his beer before allowing the heart attack to take his life. Yet, there in front of us was the half-drunk beer. Maybe not evidence that would stand up in court, but it sure as hell would stand up in a bar.

We spun around to see if we were in time to catch the change thief, expecting him to have already vanished into the dark Chicago night.

Speed is an essential element for successful thieves. They move rapidly, silently, flowing through rooms, in and out of windows, down drainpipes, up and over walls and fences, never to be seen nor heard from again. If transportation is required, it takes the form of a sporty getaway car. Or maybe a helicopter, large power boat, or Jet Ski—but in any event, speed is always an essential element. Our thief seemed to be utterly unaware of this rule. Perhaps he had never seen *The Italian Job* or *The French Connection* or maybe he was just a strong-willed independent thinker who insisted on doing things his own way. For when we spun around, he was still a good thirty feet from the door and moving at the speed of a snail.

It is rare to witness your own robbery and even rarer to have time to contemplate it. By our assessment, with the thief continuing to move at his current speed, it would take him at least another forty seconds to reach the door, and who knew how much longer to continue his disappearance into the night. Maybe as much as sixteen minutes if he was relying on the westbound 42A bus as his getaway vehicle.

Normally when a robbery is witnessed, you rely on split-second decisions. Someone shouts, "Thief! Stop him!" or "He's got my purse!" A chase may ensue—people are pushed and sometimes knocked over, resulting in, if not a capture, at least a general kafuffle. There was no need for spilt-second-decision-making with this robbery. We had all the time in the world. Perhaps a little too much time.

Rather than just acting on our immediate impulse, we had time to evaluate the situation. We were sure at least four people knew what was going on—Andrew, me, the bartender, and the thief, yet we sensed several others might also have seen this strange scenario unfold before.

We considered our options. First: right there with volume and vigor we confront the old man and demand he empty out his pockets. Second: we allow him to leave the establishment and confront him outside. And third: we call the police and have them handle it.

All of our options exhibited major flaws. Our concern with the first option was that we had no proof. Here we sat, two total strangers in a blue-collar, Polish bar about to accuse an old, fragile local man of stealing money. Even if he did turn out his pockets and lo and behold they contained exactly fourteen dollars, who could say that it was *our* fourteen dollars?

Our concern with the second option was the potential for a "Polish Pummeling." What if, when outside, the younger locals sided with the old man and dished out their own form of two-fisted justice. The only fact I knew for sure was that, if pummeled, I preferred it take place inside the bar rather than lawlessly outside, where the Geneva Convention would be far less likely to be applied. The potential pummeling made our second option look dangerous and foolhardy.

There was even concern with our third option. At the thief's current rate of knots, he would be well gone by the time the police screeched in—eager, I am sure, to delve into the hopeless case of, "Two Foreigners Missing Fourteen Dollars with No Proof and Few Friends."

A fourth option sprang to mind: embrace it. We were in the act of being robbed. Very few people ever have the opportunity to experience their own robbery in slow motion.

We sat silently on our red stools, resisting the impulse to take action, and watched quizzically as our fourteen dollars shuffled at an agonizingly slow pace out of the bar and our lives. The door slammed shut, punctuating the auto-withdrawal from our bank account. I turned slowly towards Andrew and smiled. We raised our ten-dollar bottles of beer, clinked them together, said "Cheers," drained them, and caught the next bus out of Poland.

12
HOT TO TROT

MY WALK WAS CALCULATED—a smooth saunter, perfectly paced to suggest a serious purpose, but slow enough to allow the other sun worshippers ample time to notice the arrival of this lithe, muscular, reasonably tanned newcomer to the beach. I looked straight ahead, gazing out at the deep blue Aegean Sea as if I were expecting to see my lover on the horizon, standing on the bow of a great ship with billowing white sails, her hair blowing carelessly in the wind. I donned an expression of expectation mixed with mystery and a splash of aloofness. There was no hint of a smile. Everybody knows smiles don't attract women. There's no danger in a smile.

Eight steps into my highly orchestrated arrival I was hit with the first hint of pain. Nonchalantly, I brushed it aside. I continued my seductive stroll down the beach, resisting the temptation to look around and see who was noticing this hot, available, and very hip male. Everything was running according to plan except for the pain—it was increasing. I pushed on, maintaining my casual countenance. Nothing could steal my moment in the spotlight.

My first involuntary physical movement occurred when I was midway down the beach. It was as if my brain had been telling me that something was wrong, but I hadn't been getting the message. So my body decided to see if it could help get the message across. My body's choice was simple. It stopped, raised my right foot eight inches off the scorching sand, and shook it violently. The message it was sending was now abundantly clear, "You bloody fool. Your feet are on fire."

OH MY GOD! HOT, HOT! THE PAIN! WHAT WAS I THINKING?! My right foot shot down and up came my left foot, shaking wildly as if to put out the flames. Hopping from foot to foot was an extraordinary departure from the suave stroll I had planned, especially since I started to utter short, sharp verbal alarms. Some were just noises. Others were attempts at swear words but were expelled so quickly that only the beginning of each word came out. In time with my frantically hopping feet, I screamed, "Hol—Sh—! Fu—! Ah—! Wo—the fu—! Ah—! Go—Da—! Ma—Fu—!"

My brain kicked in. "Move Matthew or be reduced to cinders!" As Sod's Law would have it, I was exactly halfway down the beach. I looked back up the beach, then out at the cool surf. "To the water!" At full speed, I hopped, jumped, and skipped, every spastic movement accompanied by a fragment of a swear word. If getting people to notice me had been my goal, I was achieving it beyond my wildest dreams.

By the time I arrived at the edge of the sea, I was completing entire swear words with proper diction. I stopped when the cool water reached an inch or so above my ankles and rocked side to side and from foot to foot as the pain slowly subsided. I contemplated the irreparable damage the scorching sand had caused to my feet, imagining blisters large enough to make me float.

My back was to the beach; slowly I rocked around and looked up. It was impossible for me not to notice that every single person in Greece was looking directly at me. I stood there awkwardly for a moment looking back. I shrugged. Then smiled.

13
HEATHER

ALTHOUGH AWAY from the comforts of home, my mother was happy to be in Scotland. I'm sure she wasn't happy to be dying. Scotland held many joyful early memories for Sylvia, most especially, love, friendship, and a connection with the rugged beauty of The Highlands.

Some people seem to breeze their way through life. Some plod methodically. For others, life is a constant struggle. My mother had been a constant struggler. However, her early years in Scotland, while serving in the British Army, seemed easier for her—a fact supported by the old sepia photos my sisters and I thumbed our way through after my mother was gone. Again and again, I found myself gazing down at a picture of Mum, sixty years younger, with the happiest of smiles radiating from the worn photographs.

As I sat next to my mother's bed in the tiny Dingwall village hospital on that September afternoon, the conversation turned towards the topic of heather and how she would love to see the beautiful Scottish heather just one more time. I felt overwhelming helplessness during the latter stages of my mother's terminal illness. Human conditioning demanded that I help—that I do something. Anything. Since I had no control over the dire circumstances, my mind desperately searched for an outlet to assist in any way I could. This need to help was critically important for my own personal survival during this painful period and at times even overshadowed the simple need to support my mother with her inevitable non-survival.

When I heard my mother's dying wish—to see heather one more time—it was as if I had just seen a green light. I had permission to start, to do something. I was no longer helpless.

Of course, being English as opposed to Scottish and having lived in America for nineteen years created an impediment to the execution of my plan. After consultation with my very Scottish brother-in-law, Donald McNiven, I quickly discovered that my basic heather knowledge was indeed abysmal. Dingwall is in the county of Ross and Cromarty. Perthshire, some two-and-a-half hours to the south, is where the heather happens.

To make matters worse, the heather had already happened, or "peaked" as they say, four to six weeks earlier. Still, I was not to be swayed from my mission. I adopted the battle cry of, "Any heather is better than no heather at all!"

Don agreed to drive me around to a few of the local areas that might still have some remnants of heather left. We headed off into the hills along narrow, winding country lanes with hedgerows as high as the car, twisting our way upwards in the pursuit of our noble cause. The higher we climbed, the more exposed we were. I could feel the car being buffeted by the gusting wind, accompanied by just enough freezing rain to complicate the already tricky decision of low wipe, intermittent wipe, or off.

We arrived at the top of Knockfarrel. I sat in the warmth of the car and surveyed my inhospitable surroundings. The wind blew hard enough to move every piece of coarse grass. The bracken was laid flat. Even the few stunted trees that had endured centuries of this climate swayed in painful resignation to their unfortunate location.

The only stationary objects were the craggy grey outcrops of granite rock, hard and impervious to all The Highlands could throw at them. The dark skies churned in rolling perpetual motion, forcing dull shadows to perform a reluctant dance as they clung to every contour of the rugged landscape. Occasionally sleeting rain moved across in horizontal sheets, as if in a great hurry to hit and freeze anything that moved. As the windows fogged and iced up, I peered out in a desperate attempt to locate heather.

What is it about The Highlands of Scotland? I wondered. The place is desolate, the weather awful, and yet as I looked out of that car window, I could think of no other place on earth where I would rather be. There is something about The Highlands that pulls me in. It's hard to put my finger on it. I think it is one of those rare places on earth that takes me back. It's primitive. Raw. Uncluttered. Time moves slower. Survival becomes more important than the next cell phone call or where the next dollar will come from.

I don't go to Scotland seeking this. It just happens to me while I'm there. By the time I leave, I attach importance to things like the friendliness of the Highlanders, the warmth of an auger in the kitchen where my clothes are drying, the tiredness in my legs from hiking hills or golf courses, and the comfortable feeling in my stomach, which is home to a fine, single malt. Simple pleasures that make me feel at ease, at home, and alive.

We lurched to a halt as a hint of purple flashed amidst the sea of greenish grey. I zipped up my Gortex wind stopper, an overly engineered rain jacket that was 100% waterproof, breathable, with a sealed zipper, stretchable seams, and double stitching. I pulled down my cap tightly and headed out to reconnoiter. Instantly, I was soaked to the bone. I leant into the wind, struggling at a forty-five-degree angle towards the color purple.

Upon arrival, I was ecstatic to discover that my quest was over. I stood in front of a five-foot-square patch of quickly fading, extremely tired looking heather. Not exactly the glorious image likely to end up on a Highland postcard, but if you picked a piece and showed it to a

Scottish botanist, he would reluctantly have to confirm that yes this was in fact heather—albeit a crappy example.

My children are still at that beautiful and innocent age where life is simply good. One ideal they both hold close to their hearts is to love, respect, and do no harm to Mother Nature. They know not to kill bugs and spiders, not to carve their names into trees, and not to pick living things. They understand that they should just look at those marvels of nature and take a mental picture that will be with them forever. For, if they do pluck a living thing from its life source, they will be forced to watch its beauty wrinkle, shrivel, and die within days, right before their eyes.

Dismissing that, I plunged my fingers deep into the cold, dark, peaty soil—digging them quickly under the coarse roots. Then with a feverish yank and an animalistic grunt, I ripped a chunk of heather right out of the ground, as if I were ripping out the heart of the Grim Reaper himself. I held it up victorious. The sleeting rain made the soil run in small, black, icy streams down my hands and wrists. I felt no cold, no remorse. Somehow I felt justified to perform this barbaric act of brutal heather slaughter.

I returned to the car, proud of my accomplishment, and was met by my brother-in-law's wry smile, which without a single word clearly asked, "You had to do that, didn't you?"

We wound our way back down to the little Dingwall hospital. I secured a thick, white china dinner bowl. I was very conscious to fill the bowl with water before placing my trophy upon it in a futile attempt to postpone its inevitable death. Then I paraded into my mother's room, heather in hand, and presented it to her. I was met with a soft thank you and a smile, which without a single word clearly stated, "You had to do that, didn't you … Heather Killer."

14
GUESS WHAT'S IN YOUR POCKET

DUE TO THE SENSITIVE and incriminating content of this story, the names of the people and substances involved have been changed ... a little bit. Although written in the first person, any connection made between me and the character named Matthias is purely coincidental.

Like so many times before, I heard Ben Haugh, landlord of the Shore Inn, bark his famously gruff and completely unintelligible call for last orders, signaling the end to an epic Sunday lunchtime drinking session. For many years, licensing laws in England mandated that pubs could only be open during Sunday lunchtime between the hours of noon and two o'clock in the afternoon. This restrictive service, intended to foster restraint, unwittingly created one of my most sacred and beloved traditions in the whole of England: spending two hours every Sunday getting smashed at the local pub.

Public houses play an important role in the English community, far more than just a place to drink. They provide a place to gather, to talk, and to get to know each other—a social club that draws the community together. So, compressing the hours of service during lunchtime on Sunday to just two hours heightened the chances of meeting friends you might not have seen during the week. Everyone from the village showed up at some point between noon and two o'clock. Attendance was strongly advised unless you wanted to be left out and miss all the news of the previous week. It was impossible to ignore the fact that this community-minded, socially-valuable establishment also served booze.

It doesn't matter what time a bar or pub closes, there will always be a select group of people that manages to time their maximum drunkenness to the exact moment of closure. Reduce the timeframe to a mere two hours and what you have created is a challenge—a challenge that every Sunday hundreds of thousands of people throughout England were glad to take on. Of course, it wasn't an easy feat to go from church to shitfaced in 120 minutes, especially in an establishment where fifty percent of the occupants were aspiring to achieve the identical goal. This often created slow service from the bar and could throw you horribly off your rhythm, causing an unwelcome moment of sobriety.

To avoid this dilemma, customers often bought three or four rounds at a time and returned to their table, performing elaborate balancing acts. Drink set upon drink set upon drink creates a bizarre food pyramid. Except, unlike the one approved by the FDA, this one will eventually kill you.

We didn't know what Ben Haugh had actually said, but we knew what was expected of us. We spilled out of the pub into the street, engaging in some loud farewells. My good friends "Ricardo" and "Sneal" and I set off up Shore Road, away from the sea, towards the village center of East Wittering. Ten minutes later we arrived at the front of Stephens and Kaye, the estate agency where I worked and above which Sneal and I lived. We walked down the side of the building, opened the door, and climbed the twisting bare wood staircase to the first floor. A bit worse for the wear, Ricardo and I slumped down on the couch while Sneal put "Sunday Bloody Sunday" on the turntable, cranked up the volume, and flopped down next to us as we discussed our options for the afternoon.

It was during this slurred brainstorming session that Sneal came up with the suggestion of smoking some ... uh ... pop ... corn. This was another telltale sign that we were still a little snockered, since none of us normally partook in this illegal activity. But on this particular Sunday options were looking a bit slim. Plus if you listen to U2 long enough and loud enough, it drives you to a craving for the rock n' roll lifestyle. But where could we scare up some popcorn? It's not like you can just go to the store and buy it off the shelf. Then Ricardo surprised me by saying matter-of-factly, "I have a bag of popcorn at home." I was shocked and intrigued. But Bono had implied it was a good idea, so off Ricardo went.

While we waited, Sneal explained that when Ricardo's parents retired, they had purchased a small nursery and now produced and sold an assortment of vegetables. Ricardo was studying horticulture and helped with the nursery when he wasn't in school. As an experiment, he had planted some popcorn seeds in one of the compost heaps in the back of the nursery. His findings confirmed that popcorn is nothing more than a weed and grows just like one, too. He had harvested the initial crop and then uprooted the remainder of the experiment. Neither he nor his friends were particularly interested in this cash crop, so the bounty had remained hidden at home until this day.

The sound of Ricardo's footsteps on the stairs announced his return. He unceremoniously plunked a bag down on the coffee table. Sneal and I looked in disbelief. This wasn't just a flimsy plastic sandwich bag; this was a full-sized brown paper bag, a grocery sack. Ricardo's small experiment had obviously been a substantial success. This sort of volume is what they show on the national news, along with images of people being hauled off in handcuffs, their faces blurred to prevent viewers from recognizing the villains and saying, "Hey, isn't that the nice guy from the nursery?"

We knew the safest course of action was to lessen the magnitude of popcorn in our possession. Clearly, the most efficient way to reduce the quantity was through its use. To hedge our bets, we started "using" right away. Soon, the afternoon and early evening had slipped by. Ricardo had to leave but said he had no use for the bag and decided to leave it with us. We were in no condition to resist.

So for two weeks, Sneal and I auditioned for the role of habitual popcorn smokers. The only characteristic that separated us from actual users was our total lack of reverence for the popcorn itself. Not having paid for it, coupled with the sheer volume we possessed, imparted upon us a cavalier attitude. Usually, popcorn users are fastidious in their painstakingly slow assembly of a … point. They treat the popcorn as if it is gold dust while explaining all the ins and outs and dos and don'ts of good popcorn smoking etiquette. This whole ritual often overshadows the actual consumption.

Not so with us. We would lay out a few papers, grab a fistful of popcorn, throw it in the general vicinity, and hope that some landed in the appropriate spot. Our laissez-faire attitude meant that after two weeks, our entire apartment had a thin layer of popcorn coating every surface. It was all over—floors, tables, chairs, lampshades, bookcases, toaster ovens, and even our clothes. All had become lightly, fragrantly dusted. I think we knew the sooner the bag was gone the sooner we would return to our normal lives—unless during this period we signed a recording contract. What we needed to focus on was emptying the bag. So our carelessness increased, as did the apartment's herbal film.

One morning, a couple of weeks into our unconventional lifestyle, I was working downstairs in the front office of the estate agency. Two men wearing suits came in. I greeted them warmly. They looked similar to each other, as if they were a matching pair, and although you could collect them separately they would always be worth more as a set. Their faces were stern, their hair short, and their haircuts cheap. From a distance their suits imparted importance, but upon closer inspection I noticed they were ill-fitting, worn, and appeared to be more of a reluctant uniform than a demand for status.

"Good morning."

The two men swept aside my greeting with an air of authority, which made me feel these gentlemen usually got what they wanted. They started firing questions at me in rapid succession. I had the sense they were used to having their questions answered, and I felt it was best not to disappoint.

"Is the address here 17 Shore Road?"

"Yes." I refrained from pointing out that the address was clearly posted outside the estate office.

"Are you the owner?"

"I am one of the partners."

"How long have you been a partner?"

"About three years."

"Do you know Derrick Fiddler?"

Suddenly everything started to make sense. Derrick Fiddler had burst on to the scene eighteen months earlier, acting like the long-lost friend of one of my partners. He had weaseled his way into several local business ventures without ever putting up any money. He also wore a suit, but his suits were custom made with the finest silk, augmented by a crisply pressed shirt, matching silk tie, and handkerchief in his breast pocket. When not smoking cigarettes, he was talking. Talking so quickly you never had time to stop him and say, "What was that middle part again?" Derrick Fiddler's personality was energetic and persuasive. You could easily lower your guard, especially when he told you things you wanted to hear. He had disappeared about five months earlier, as mysteriously as he had arrived, leaving in his wake a trail of broken promises, bad feelings, and illegal practices. I had spent the last four months helping my partner recover and rebuild.

Now it was my turn to ask a few questions.

"To whom do I have the pleasure of speaking?" I asked in a friendly, non-confrontational tone. They both looked surprised that I had turned the tables, hesitated, and then the gentleman on the right said, "I am Detective Chief Inspector Dorkins from the Criminal Investigation Department and this is Detective Constable Johnson also from CID."

"Oh," I said, taken aback a little. I invited them into my office. We talked for half an hour. I was happy to pass along the information I had. Fiddler had hurt several people in our small community, so bringing him to justice seemed right—and it would feel really good.

Eventually Detective Dorkins said, "Mr. Fiddler's last known address is 17A Shore Road." "Yes," I said. "There's an apartment above this office in which he lived."

"Who lives there now?"

"I do."

"We should maybe take a quick look at it, if that's okay."

"Right," I said.

Then it hit me. Holy Crap! I'm inviting the CID into my illegally decorated apartment. Brilliant! Let's make Derrick Fiddler look like a choir boy, shall we? Panic overwhelmed me. I could feel the cold steel of handcuffs on my wrists and a large, heavy hand pushing my head down to prevent me from banging it as I entered the backseat of an unmarked police car. I murmured something about having a roommate and how I should make sure it is okay with him. The detectives agreed and asked if they could use my phone. I said yes and then added quickly, "Please feel free to use it as long as you'd like." I stopped myself from adding, "A really long time is fine with me. I've got some cleaning to do!"

I excused myself and walked casually out of my office. Midway through the front office, I hit overdrive. I careened out of the front door and spun around the corner, flung open my apartment door, and galloped up the stairs three at a time. The overpowering smell of trouble enveloped me. I looked in dismay around the apartment. No hard edges existed anywhere; all were softened by the rolling contours of illegal excessiveness. I dashed to the closet and grabbed our upright vacuum cleaner. The floor was first, but when my path was interrupted by my arrival at the couch, I simply muscled the Hoover up and over, vacuuming the back, arms, and cushions. *Why stop there?* I thought. I continued across the side table. It worked so well, I was encouraged. I carried on with my unconventional yet speedy cleaning method with the first ever upright vacuuming of a standard lamp. Now there was no stopping me. I had no idea the vacuum could be used on kitchen counters, appliances, windowsills, the breakfast table, and coats hanging on the back door. I even vacuumed the vacuum itself. If the cat hadn't been so nimble, she too would have had a quick going over.

Soon the apartment started to reappear from under its light green film. I continued to vacuum the stereo system, a pair of shoes, an old copy of the Chichester Observer, some junk mail, the shower, the toilet, the tub. Once satisfied, I placed what was now the most valuable vacuum cleaner in the whole of England deep into the closet. I flung open windows and hit every room with a massive blast of air freshener. I composed myself at the top of the stairs, wiped a bead of sweat from my forehead, and was just about to return to my office when I noticed I had left the large brown bag of popcorn sitting in the middle of the living room table. I grabbed it, compressing it into a grapefruit-sized ball. Looking around frantically for a place to hide the contraband, I opened the closet door and stuffed the bag of popcorn deep into the pocket of one of Sneal's suit jackets.

Intense pressure causes snap decisions with no regard for full analysis. One factor percolates to the surface—self-preservation. My jacket hung next to Sneal's, yet there I was saving my own arse stuffing drugs into my best friend's pocket.

I descended the stairs and breezed cheerily into my office. The most senior detective was still on the phone. *Thank goodness he read my thoughts.* Karen, my assistant, had come out of her office and was engaged in casual conversation with the other detective. Our eyes met and she gave me the, "What the hell's going on?" look. I then realized it had not been a long phone conversation at all.

The call had just started. The inadequate soundproofing in these old buildings meant the CID had been subject to the deafening noise of my frantic twelve-and-a-half minute multi-surface vacuuming.

He hung up the phone and we headed towards the apartment. As we walked, I noticed that the two officers gave each other a knowing glance as if to say, "Just follow Mr. Clean Freak who's a bit too particular about the appearance of his precious apartment." At the top of the stairs our nostrils were assaulted by a chemist's attempt to simulate the smell of a bouquet of alpine flowers. To play the role in which I imagined they had cast me, I considered asking them to remove their unpolished, scuffed shoes. They poked their heads in the front door, gave the scene a quick cursory glance, turned around, said, "Righty, ho, then," and walked out. That was it? I'd worked so hard I half-considered inviting them in.

As they descended the stairs and disappeared from view, I became aware of a strange sensation. I realized it was my heart pounding. Its rate dropped steadily from the 160 beats per minute it had sustained for the last agonizingly painful twenty minutes of my life.

That evening as Sneal and I sat on our well-vacuumed couch, I retold the events of the day in great detail. Sneal was very impressed with the way I had handled myself under such pressure. Finally when all was said and done, he looked at me and said in a matter-of-fact tone, "So, Matthias, where *is* the bag of popcorn?"

15
THE BAKED ALASKA

IT WASN'T UNTIL I WORKED in a restaurant that I became aware of the complex twists and turns necessary to successfully deliver food to table, all with the nonchalant swagger of an overly confident waiter.

After skiing the winter away in the pristine glory of Crested Butte, high in the majestic Rocky Mountains, my friend Andrew and I recognized the unavoidable approach of spring and, along with it, unemployment due to the seasonal closure of Penelope's Restaurant where we were waiters. Ready for a new adventure and needing the work, we headed south, way south, in search of sun, beaches, and fruity cocktails with umbrellas.

We spent our first days in Key West proudly parading our "skier tans" around the local beaches. Our handsomely bronzed faces, necks, and hands were perfectly happy to be exposed to the fierce sun. Unfortunately, the remainder of our previously unexposed ghostly white flesh was not as happy. Our skin proceeded to sizzle, bubble, and burn, causing us intense pain that even the concentrated consumption of fruity cocktails with umbrellas failed to dent. I looked suspiciously at my bottle of Coppertone Sport High Performance UVA/UVB Broad Spectrum SPF 50 sunscreen and discovered its only flaw. It has to be applied. The only sunscreen that has ever truly protected me from getting sunburns has a much shorter name. A job.

Andrew and I secured gainful employment as waiters at The Quay restaurant. We relied on our English accents, far more than our skillset, during the interview. Words like "wonderful," "jolly good," and "so terribly sorry I don't have a social security number" kept popping out.

Key West is famous for many things—being the southernmost point of the continental United States, it offers breathtaking sunsets and Ernest Hemingway spending an inordinate amount of time smashed out of his gourd at Sloppy Joe's on Duval Street.

I am fully aware I have not mentioned Jimmy Buffet.

The sunsets, it has to be said, are truly spectacular. The viewing spot of choice is Mallory Square. It is here at sunset—the exact time of which, to the minute, is advertised, broadcasted, posted, heralded, and tattooed on the forehead of every sorry t-shirt shop employee—that thousands of people gather to ooh and aah at nature's natural fireworks display.

It always amazes me that when confronted with natural beauty the normal human response is to all flock to it and view the spectacle while surrounded by strangers all crushed together. As much as we humans struggle to get along, we sure do gravitate towards each other in moments like these.

At the designated time every evening a mass of tourists would gather with the singular goal of seeing the sun set. The sun, bless its heart, never let them down and right on cue slowly sank gloriously into the Gulf of Mexico. The sun's disappearance created a unique situation. One moment there were 2,500 happy people with a purpose and then a second later all 2,500 people had achieved their goal simultaneously, leaving them a little lost. This created an odd shifting within the crowd, almost as if the physical movement was attached to the mental struggle of how to fill the void.

Luckily, humans are the smartest species on planet Earth, so all 2,500 people seemed to arrive at the exact same conclusion at exactly the same time. Let's eat! The tourists followed their stomachs and marched en masse to the top of Duval Street, as if every restaurant had hired Ivan Pavlov to ring the dinner bell. They then salivated their hungry selves straight down the street.

The very first restaurant they saw was The Quay. Sweet location if you happen to be a restaurant owner or a waiter with a masochistic bent. The Quay actually hired people to stand outside and herd the sea of drooling tourists into the premises. Moments before the sun set, seven or eight people dined peacefully in The Quay with all twenty-two wait staff quietly watching. Fifteen minutes later, all twenty-two wait staff were madly rushing around with six or seven tables, each filled with sunset-satisfied, yet extremely hungry and demanding tourists.

The wait staff was split evenly—eleven men and eleven women. The men, however, were not split evenly. Nine were gay, leaving Andrew and me as the only two straight males. It is often said that gay waiters are the very best waiters. Andrew and I offered no challenge to that axiom. The intense pressure created by five hundred diners all arriving simultaneously made me often wish I was gay.

You would think that given these circumstances the owners would have been wise to create an easy-to-present menu with limited items. Not so. The menu at The Quay best resembled an IKEA catalog. Page after page, it went on and on. So, just when the customer decided on chicken for their evening meal, they noticed on page 247 that we also offered dried yak breast with a sautéed goat spleen topped with a recently deceased waiter. Oh! How could anyone resist! Then the whole table would engage in an in-depth conversation as to the cholesterol levels in dried yak breast. We even offered Chateaubriand, carved tableside. And for dessert, Bananas Foster and Baked Alaska. Desserts, by the way, that must be set on fire.

One evening, Andrew hurriedly approached me in the kitchen. His eyes rolled to the back of his head with an "I need this like a hole in the head" expression on his face.

"Table 15, they just ordered a bloody Baked Alaska. I've never done one."

It was from this point that a horrible chain of events unfolded and culminated in what could only be described as one of "The Waiter's Hall of Fame Most Memorable Moments of All Time."

I had served my first Baked Alaska a few nights earlier, during a much slower time. It wasn't exactly pretty, but I got through it and lived to tell the tale. So I felt qualified to help Andrew, despite his unease.

I don't know why it's called a Baked Alaska. In all the time I spent around the dessert, the "baking" was pretty much conspicuous in its absence. Basically, the beast has a crust and ice cream base with a frozen meringue top. You cover it liberally with 151 rum and then flame it when served. My instructions to Andrew were thus: "Run to the freezer, grab a Baked Alaska, which is pre-frozen in a glass dish, put the dish on a salad plate, go to the bar, and get a shot of 151 rum. Just before you arrive at the table, douse the Baked Alaska with the 151, present with a flair, then flambé the dessert, voila! Very impressive. Guaranteed 20% tip. Nothing to it."

He grabbed a salad plate from the prep stack. (In retrospect, my instructions could be criticized for not informing Andrew to remove the paper doily from the salad plate before the Baked Alaska was placed on it. Perhaps I assumed that when dealing with fire, the removal of any delicate paper product from the general vicinity would be a given.)

Oblivious of this slip, Andrew headed for the bar, where love would serve him a cruel blow. Debbie was a rotund, jolly, bartending professional. Without a doubt, she was our favorite. For starters, she was as sharp as a tack. For example, she quickly discovered a remedy when a mistake was made at the bar, such as adding tonic instead of soda to a drink. Rather than throw it away, Debbie realized that summoning two Englishmen had a similar effect to utilizing the large drain. Drinks would disappear down our throats without a trace. As you can imagine, a large busy restaurant such as The Quay produced a very satisfactory amount of mistakes.

Given this wonderful working relationship, Andrew and I became fast friends with Debbie. And Debbie became friends with me. With Andrew, however, she wanted much more than friendship. Her lusty eyes followed him around the restaurant. The crush was extreme, but so was the number of free drinks coming my way. So I encouraged Debbie in her pursuit of Andrew while we continued our experimentation, or rather research, on cocktails one would otherwise never actually serve or even try. Such as a Vodka Scotch.

This was all well and good until Andrew hurriedly approached Debbie and requested the shot of 151 rum. Debbie viewed this request as a wanton advance. If Andrew was drinking 151 (which, incidentally, is 75% pure alcohol), along with all the other drinks she had given him, what chance would he have at refusing her late-night advances? But to be absolutely sure, she was extra generous with the 151. Many would say, more than generous. As in, what's the difference, really, between a double shot and a triple? Andrew left the bar hurriedly, heading towards Doomed Table 15, armed with his goblet of rocket fuel. Debbie's adoring eyes followed him as usual; only this time, they had an unmistakable hint of optimism.

Sensing that the precious commodity of time was passing him by, Andrew arrived in the vicinity of Table 15 at a full run. He then performed the classic waiter "pause." Three feet away he screeched to a halt, regained his composure, and sauntered up as if he had all the time in the world. With his back slightly turned away from the table, Andrew sloshed the fuel over the dessert, then promptly turned and elegantly presented the Baked Alaska.

It is roughly at this point in such a dramatic dining moment that the male guest usually talks to his female companion. Only couples order these fancy delights because flaming desserts fall into the genre of "Go Directly to Bed" desserts.

It is important that before the death-defying feat is attempted, the man builds the necessary anticipation. Andrew's gentleman customer leaned across Table 15 towards his soon-to-be-bedded date. His expensive, perfectly pressed shirt was unbuttoned one button too far and his oily, suspiciously jet-black hair was groomed to perfection. A sly smile crept across his face as he said seductively, "Now comes the fire, Baby."

His date, slightly aroused, lightly licked her voluptuous red painted lips. Her lithe Jazzercised body shifted slightly in her seat while she unconsciously tapped her six-and-a-half-inch stiletto-heeled right foot in rhythm with her quickening heart.

Much like a matador drawing a sword in preparation for the slaughter of the bull, Andrew drew a match, and with one flowing stroke, lit it. With great authority, he slowly lowered the match towards the dessert. His masterful show began to unravel when the match got about eight inches from the Baked Alaska. The fumes from the sheer quantity of 151 Rocket Fuel were enough for the whole thing to explode. Up it went. A three-foot column of fiery spectacle lit up the restaurant accompanied by the unmistakable WHOOOSH of overzealous combustion.

The poor customer, who only moments before had been so confidently explaining what to expect, almost dislocated his neck trying to get out of the way of the inferno. Thoughts flooded his mind, ranging from a general concern for singeing eyebrows to some vague recollection of the movie *The Towering Inferno*. As quickly as the column of fire rose, it diminished and settled into a manageable eight- to twelve-inch, steadily burning, bluish-orange flame.

The desired effect had been achieved. And I thought, "Wow. Andrew has actually gotten away with it." I could see that Andrew's expression said, "Well, that was a little bit more than I expected, but I'm out of the woods now." The dessert continued to burn, allowing time for the couple to gaze into the flames and into each other's eyes. Other diners at nearby tables mouthed to their fellow guests, "That's a Baked Alaska," in case a less worldly member of their table was surprised by the sudden volcanic activity in Key West.

There exists a thin line between interest and irritation. A flaming dessert is an excellent way to examine just where that line is drawn. The Baked Alaska was still burning with the stamina of a Hemingway cocktail party. It quickly sailed past the point of interest and became an irritating "I Can't Exactly Eat My Expensive Dessert While It's Flaming" kind of moment. Andrew, sensing this, did what any good waiter would do; he began gently fanning with both hands back and forth across the dessert. This proved highly ineffective.

The burning meringue dripped onto the delicate paper doily, causing a secondary fire to encircle the main event. Andrew quickly realized that a more direct approach was required. Along with this realization came his first rolling wave of panic. It was at this point that Andrew engaged in an activity commonly known in waiting circles as "Not a Good Thing to Do." Specifically, blowing on your customer's food. Whether it was the ever-rising tide of panic or just a practical English moment that drove Andrew to this, we will never know.

It started with a sheepish little puff out of the corner of his mouth. When this meek effort produced no results whatsoever, Andrew decided it had become opening day of "International Blow on Other People's Food Season." He continued to blow. At first he still attempted to do it surreptitiously, but as the desired result failed to materialize, the blowing became more and more blatant.

With ever-increasing velocity, again and again, he blew. Now Andrew was gulping in huge amounts of air and exhaling with such force that every attempt registered a five or six on the Beaufort Wind Scale. By now the dessert was a mass of steadily burning molten sugar over increasingly runny ice cream, encircled by the charred remnants of a paper doily.

At a time of crisis, the mind often narrows so as to allow total focus on only the immediate. Nothing is allowed to cloud the objective. Consequently, Andrew had excluded everything from his consciousness except the blazing dessert. Nothing else existed. He grabbed the dessert in his hand and, holding it in front of his customer, filled his lungs to capacity. With his mouth only inches from the fire, he let out a stream of air so powerful that something had to give. And give it did.

The molten meringue top launched off the softened ice cream and relocated itself squarely in the middle of the customer's chest; a mass of syrupy burning sugar. And lest we forget, sugar burns hot. Andrew's eyes widened as did every other pair in the restaurant. With his customer now on fire, Andrew didn't waste a second. He followed his instincts. He leaned over and slapped the man in the middle of the chest in the desperate hope that he could snuff out the sugary flames that were burning a hole in his customer's shirt.

It is rare, indeed, for a waiter to visit the "Waiter's List of Not Good Things to Do" so frequently. To visit twice in such rapid succession is almost unheard of. First, setting your customer on fire is never popular. Second, hitting your customer will rarely smooth things over. Unfortunately, all the slap did was splatter the fiery mess. The fire was removed from the chest of the customer, but unfortunately the burning meringue had now separated into lots of small fireballs, creating multiple sugar fires burning all over Table 15 and its occupants. Andrew slapped frantically at every fire, which made each divide and multiply into more tiny sugar fires. Both customers exhibited an excellent sense of survival and joined in the mad slapping. Soon the entire table bore a resemblance to a squad of energetic teenagers at a Whack-a-Mole tournament.

All of sudden, as quickly as the disaster had started, the fire was out. There was an eerie silence. A stillness swept across the entire restaurant. Table 15 smoldered. It was reminiscent of a post-battle scene in an old war movie. A slight mist drifting. A muffled noise. A charred smoking stump. An ominous sense that something bad had happened here.

Andrew gathered himself. He picked up the charred remains of the Baked Alaska and then presented it, saying, in his most proper English accent, "Sir, Madam. Please, enjoy your dessert."

With that said, he promptly turned, re-stiffened his upper lip, and kissed his 20% tip goodbye.

16
HOW BIG IS YOUR TRUCK?

THE ONLY THING BIGGER than a Super Target is a Super Target parking lot. On a Saturday afternoon, my family and I found ourselves dwarfed once again by the familiar sea of asphalt and its maze of white lines. We were engaged in the ever slow and painful process of inserting small children into a motor vehicle while burdened with the fruits of shopping, when a huge truck turned into the lot and accelerated at a speed most NASCAR drivers would envy.

I describe the truck as huge, but in reality it was a standard three-quarter-ton pickup truck with colossal wheels that came up to my chin. I would like to describe it as a monster truck, but I am unclear as to when a truck with large wheels ceases to be just a truck with large wheels and qualifies for the mythical title of Monster

Truck. Perhaps the transformation occurs when the aspiring vehicle obtains sponsorship from Red Bull.

The truck turned into our row and roared towards us.

It's rare, but there *are* times in life when it is better to speak out than it is to care about what you are actually saying.

If the intent is to convey general concern, this can be done with tone and pace alone. The actual choice of words is almost incidental. For my wife, this was one such occasion. I fully supported her action, and even to some degree, her choice of words. While Maitland was climbing into the car, Alastair had drifted towards the rear of the car and was temporarily out of our view. The truck was tearing towards us at Mach Nine. The startling velocity combined with his super-sized wheels meant the driver would stand little chance of noticing a short, blonde, three-year-old. An alarm needed to be raised. And raised quickly. My wife took to the task immediately, bellowing out for all in a two-mile radius to hear, "Alastair! Watch out for that big ass truck!"

Not exactly poetry, but extremely effective nonetheless. Alastair stayed put. The truck roared by without incident. Within a few seconds, we were back to the labor of gathering up Alastair and placing him into our car.

After several minutes of driving, we drew out of the Super Target parking lot and were headed home. It surprised me how quiet Alastair was in the backseat. Since silence usually means something seriously bad is happening, I glanced back to check. As I turned, my eyes fell upon a young boy deep in thought. He wore a quizzical

expression, as if he was trying to piece together something that just didn't quite fit. We continued to drive for a
while longer in silence.

Then, out of the blue, Alastair spoke up. In a slow
and deliberate voice, almost measured—as if he'd spent
time rehearsing how he would pose this important question—he asked, "Mum, how big *is* an Ass Truck?"

17
FOOD FOR THOUGHT

I FEEL A STRANGER'S HAND in my pocket but react too slowly. Helpless, I watch the thief dart into a crowded European marketplace. He vanishes as he's absorbed into the ebb and flow of the crowd. He stole my wallet, but he also stole part of me, a fragment of my life. Panic and anger peak and eventually subside, giving way to empty bitterness and disappointment.

Thirty years later, I feel the same. Once again, I am being robbed.

The tension in my shoulders increases as the overwhelming feeling of too-much-to-do-with-not-enough-time-to-do-it suffocates me. Anxiously, I keep one eye on the road and the other on the digital clock Honda has provided on my dash. In a blink the numbers change. I accelerate in a feeble attempt to outpace time. Time: the supreme pickpocket. It steals the minutes of my life that I carelessly let slip through my fingers.

I lurch the minivan to a stop in my driveway. I am scheduled to work an open house in less than an hour and I have yet to shower and shave. I only recently earned my real estate license and do not want to be late. Before the doors of the van open I look at my daughter, still buckled into the passenger seat, and break the silence that has blanketed us during our journey. "I need a favor," I plead. She looks back at me sleepy-eyed, with unkempt hair, her face drawn and tired—hallmarks of a sleepless sleepover. While hastily exiting the vehicle, I continue in a part persuasive, part desperate tone, "Can you *please* make me a sandwich while I'm in the shower so I can take it to work with me? I'm running horribly late." She answers curtly. "Dad, you're killing me."

I don't have time to argue with a soon-to-be teen. I head into the house and straight to the bathroom, imagining that her response actually means, "Yes, Father. Gladly."

My ablutions complete, I dress, grab my briefcase, and head through the kitchen towards the back door. My daughter's voice stops me in my tracks. "Here you go, Dad." Maitland holds out the orange lunchbox I have sent her to school with for the last six years.

Well before any inkling of children, my wife and I purchased a home one block away from Edison Elementary School. We were much relieved when we discovered how a single block was far enough to be out of earshot of the annoying high-pitched screams and squeals that accompany every recess. It wasn't until the birth of our children that I fully appreciated the advantages of our location. The simple act of walking my kids that one block to school during their early years enriched my life deeply. The leisurely stroll every day gave me an opportunity to be present, listen, and parent; it allowed me to catch the loose threads of time and weave them into the fabric of our lives.

The only downside to being merely a block away was that by third grade, Maitland, my eldest, had deemed my role as escort redundant. Not only did she walk herself to school, but she also ably chaperoned her younger brother, Alastair. I had been given a pink slip by my eight-year-old daughter.

Despite the change in my duties, our new routine became as comfortable as a worn pair of slippers. I kissed my scholars goodbye in the kitchen. I watched as they trudged out the back door, across the patio, down the driveway, and out of view. A moment later, unable to resist, I retraced their steps and arrived at the sidewalk with enough delay to remain unnoticed. I didn't want to molly-coddle my children, but I couldn't help it. My children had moved on, grown up, but I hadn't.

I still needed to feel needed. I still longed to walk with them to school, travelling through our lives together, side-by-side in actual time. Now unable to do this, I compromised. I secretly watched over them from afar.

Two small figures—one tall, one short, both with hair still wet—walked side-by-side in the distance, a third of their bodies concealed by giant backpacks that rocked gently back and forth to the rhythm of their gait. Attached to each figure was a lunch box; one green, one orange, each containing love, hope, and belief in the future.

Every step of their journey took my children further away from me. But as they shrank into the distance, with every step, their independence and confidence grew. These were qualities I had strived to instill in my children. It was bittersweet watching my children bravely walk to school, as I knew that short walk would encourage them to travel even further from me in the future.

Now, here stands my daughter, handing me her orange lunch box. I hug her tightly and enthusiastically whisper in her ear, "Thank you. I …" She interrupts my lovey-dovey show of appreciation by replying in an affected adult voice, "Now go. Hurry or you'll be late." I stumble out of the house, briefcase in one hand, lunchbox in the other, and, thanks to my daughter, back on schedule.

A few hours later a flash of lightning, followed by a crack of thunder, herald a storm's arrival. The driving rain causes a lull in visitors to my open house. The solitude gives me the opportunity to eat the sandwich my daughter made for me. I place the little orange lunchbox on the empty kitchen counter and unzip it. I fold back the top to reveal not only the neatly prepared ham, cheese, and tomato sandwich in a Tupperware container, but also a small snack-sized Ziploc bag full of salt n' vinegar chips, a strawberry yogurt with a spoon, and two homemade brownies brought home from the sleepover.

I smile as love for my daughter wells up inside me. I had known that if I spent time with my children—loving, caring, and teaching them—one day, if I was lucky, they would return the favor. I just hadn't realized it would start so soon.

18
THE RIGHT HONORABLE DIP

LATE ONE NIGHT, after an evening of extreme merriment with my college friends, I found myself in the kitchen of the Right Honorable Mrs. Burn. Her kitchen was graciously appointed, boasting a flagstone floor, handcrafted hardwood cabinetry, exquisite lighting, and a plethora of shiny commercial-grade appliances that were to be expected from any Right Honorable Kitchen. The sheer opulence and comfort screamed, "Don't just cook in me, live in me."

Mrs. Burn was not present. I was with five of my Chichester College friends, one of whom was Rory Burn, son of the Right Honorable. We were playing catch with raw eggs that the Right Honorable stainless steel refrigerator had generously offered up. Eggs flew around the kitchen as we tossed with gay abandon. After the catching part of the game failed on several occasions, Rory wisely thought it best to extricate his playful guests from the house before we caused irreparable damage or awoke his mother who was asleep upstairs.

He opened French doors at the rear of the house and we tumbled out onto a gracious flagstone patio lit by a partial moon and as many stars as could peek out from behind the scudding clouds. Adjoining the patio was a large swimming pool.

Water has always attracted me, especially late-night water. I lived on the Chichester Channel, so after-hours skinny dipping occurred quite frequently. Less frequently enjoyed was the luxury of heated water, especially heated water owned by nobility. My powers to resist melted away into a puddle. I hastily pulled off my clothes and created a neat pile near the edge of the pool. I topped off the heap with my boxer shorts, took two quick steps, and launched. For a split second I hung above the glassy surface completely dry, but 100% committed. In a breath, the water enveloped me. I struggled to adapt to the sudden change in temperature. Still submerged, I sensed a second impact a moment after mine as the larger frame of Andrew displaced a greater volume of water than I had. Simultaneously, we popped to the surface, whipping the hair out of our eyes with a quick flick of the neck.

No matter how heated a swimming pool is it always takes my breath away. Once the air rushes back into my body my next reaction is a loud involuntary roar. Andrew and I roared in unison then glided around the pool, experiencing that untethered feeling of naked swimming, absolutely nothing between the water and my skin. The absence of swimming trunks created weightless freedom in the personal area I so commonly restrict. I enjoy the sensation; however, my self-consciousness means I prefer to experience it in the dark.

Andrew and I were the only two who had opted for a swim, but I could make out my other friends huddled near the edge of the pool chatting and laughing. My body adjusted to the water temperature, and I settled in to enjoy my late-night dip. Two strong strokes propelled me through the velvety water, creating ripples in the inky black surface.

All of a sudden, I heard the click of a switch immediately followed by the igniting pop of halogen lamps. The entire rear patio and pool flooded with light. To make matters worse, three sump lights burst on inside the pool, illuminating Andrew and me from beneath in all our glory.

Our raucous enjoyment of the pool had awoken the Right Honorable Mrs. Burn, who was now standing above us on her bedroom balcony. I expected Rory to step forward and make a quick apology to his mother, initiating a swift return to darkness. But Rory panicked. Before his mother saw him, he dashed out of the circle of light and darted into the darkness of the garden, without saying a word. Andrew and I had never met the Right Honorable Mrs. Burn. So with no reassurance from her son, she now thought she had a couple of hooligans swimming naked in her pool.

She scolded us from her perch, using exceptionally haughty tones of a well-bred English lady. Her accent was so affected that neither of us could fully understand what she was saying. Rather than ask for a translation we felt it better to implement a speedy exit. Andrew threw caution to the wind, heaved himself out of the pool, grabbed his clothes, and high-tailed it towards the ditch at the end of the garden. I was about to emulate his smooth escape, when I noticed Neal heading to my rescue out of the gloom. Relief swept through me at the sight of my trusted friend.

I held up my right hand so he could help pull me out. Neal reached my pile of clothes and scooped them up. I further extended my arm in anticipation. Water dripped from each outstretched fingertip as I readied myself to grip the hand of my savior. He moved within inches of me. As I looked up I could see my clothes passing over my head, flying in slow motion towards the center of the pool. As they settled gently on the surface I saw Neal turn and sprint away from the pool's edge, his laughter a taunting cackle as he disappeared into the darkness.

Stunned, I jolted back into real time. I pulled my naked body out of the pool and sprinted to the ditch. Without inspection I jumped in. There to greet me were thick brambles with sharp thorns and a half-dressed Andrew laughing loud enough to wake up a whole neighborhood of Right Honorables. We huddled in the ditch, hopeful the floodlights would be turned off so I could sneak back to retrieve my clothes, but no such luck. The lights continued to illuminate the now tranquil pool. The evidence of recent activity floated grotesquely in the middle of the pool, resembling a dismembered corpse. It would take a braver man than I to mount a recovery operation under full floodlights, plus I had an ominous sense that the authorities would soon arrive. My clothes seemed like a small price to pay for my freedom.

Rory and the others had long since vanished. Andrew was kind enough to divvy up some of his clothes so I could wear more than just brambles. Reluctantly, he relinquished his boxer shorts, shirt, and socks, while maintaining ownership of the good bits—his jeans, shoes, and cap. Careful to stay out of the light, we snuck around to the front of the house. We tiptoed our way through the lush grass, flower beds, and shrubbery. Two men, one bare-chested, one bare-legged, furtively moved through the shadows. The light in the kitchen snapped on. Spurred on, we gained speed as we scrunched across the gravel driveway towards the car. Andrew took bold purposeful steps, while I hopped and lurched behind him, my stocking feet punished by the sharp stones. We leapt into Andrew's car. He turned the key, forcing the engine to life just as the porch light came on. With spinning wheels and spitting gravel we sped away rapidly, thankful to be wrapping our half-naked bodies in the thick, safe blanket of night.

As we drove, I pictured Rory the following morning perched at the granite counter top, listening to his mother's explanation of what had happened the night before. While feigning utter surprise and disgust, I envisioned his response. "No. Really? Oh, unbelievable, Mother. What riff-raff." A little ways down the road we passed two police cars heading at high speed in the opposite direction. I smiled as I imagined three bumbling bobbies going fishing for my clothes.

19
CANDLE IN THE WIND

I LOVE THE SUMMER HOLIDAYS because I get to spend all day every day with my kids. The only drawback to summer holidays is I have to spend all day every day with my kids. Please don't get me wrong. I love my children more than anything on earth, but as the summer drags on I occasionally find that there isn't quite enough absence to make my heart grow fonder.

During one particular summer, it was decided that the lucky kiddos would attend Camp Matthew—also known as the "I'm-Your-Father-Who's-Too-Cheap-to-Send-You-to-a-Real-Camp" camp. Those who have committed to a similar undertaking will appreciate the considerable effort it takes to constantly come up with new and exciting adventures for each fun-filled summer camp day. It is not long before your judgment becomes a little skewed. What you believe will be a scintillating day of fun, as seen through the ever critical eyes of your children, is not. Like for example, watching other people, aka strangers, play tennis at City Park, or perhaps a quick tour of the frozen food aisle at Safeway.

Naturally, towards the end of the summer holidays one is reduced to some slim pickings for fun. It was during that phase of their summer holidays when I came up with this latest cracker of an adventure—a trip to the Mother Cabrini Shrine. It's a little known fact that all kids appreciate a good pilgrimage to a Catholic shrine. They just don't know it. So with great reluctance, my two summer campers boarded the minivan, departing on what only I perceived to be a fabulous adventure with outstanding potential.

The Mother Cabrini Shrine is located in the foothills about ten miles to the west of Denver. The amazing Mother Cabrini founded sixty-seven hospitals, orphanages, and schools during her lifetime. In 1902, she came upon the property near Denver and seven years later negotiated the purchase to make it into a summer camp for local orphans. It was there in 1912 that Mother Cabrini performed a miracle by creating a spring that gurgled out of the arid mountainside. The spring exists to this day, and you can drink its cool, slightly sulfuric healing waters. Many faithful fill plastic containers and return home equipped with gallons of this precious, holy liquid.

On arrival I smiled, congratulating myself for creating the perfect outing—a little physical exercise, a touch of history, and a momentary exploration of spirituality.

We exited the smoothly gliding doors of the minivan, grabbed our water bottles, which were filled with non-miraculous Denver tap water, and headed for the steps. We were greeted by clear blue skies and a chilly, boisterously playful wind—a frequent visitor to the Denver foothills. The shrine of Mother Cabrini perches on top of a steep hill, crowned with a beautiful twenty-two-foot-tall white statue. The only access to the shrine is by way of 373 steps that climb through prayerful gardens, Stations of the Cross, and thin air.

We headed up step after step, trudging against the wind, admiring the gardens, and occasionally reading the little plaques set amid the plants and flowers commemorating loved ones. We were surrounded by peace, and I was surprised at how quickly the children sensed we were in a special place. On several occasions, I looked up ahead and saw my children standing side-by-side on the steps above me, quietly contemplating a plaque with a name and a date. For one tender fleeting moment, we were all removed from this complicated world.

Around step number 64, I realized the problem with 373 steps is that there are 373 of them. As much as you may think it's just something you take in stride, it still involves 373 strides, one after the other. Each one ceaselessly elevating you by seven inches. I am a relatively fit man, yet I could feel my heart rate rising and my knees fatiguing as I continued to be physically challenged. I couldn't help but wonder how many of these small brass plaques honored the elderly faithful who started out on this prayerful ascent only to succumb to the physical rig-

or and promptly die. I imagined hearing the hushed yet urgent voice of a nun, "Quick, Sister, there's another one down! Grab a plaque!" I imagined a slightly flustered group of nuns rolling the limp body off the steps, into a shallow grave, while planting a quick columbine and a suitable brass reminder.

As we neared the statue at the summit, I was puzzled to see that Mother Cabrini appeared to have a very healthy beard. I was aware that bearded ladies played a prominent role in circuses but was less familiar with their impact in monastic life. With each step my concern grew, until we got close enough for me to realize that the twenty-two-foot bearded figure was in fact not Mother Cabrini, but the well-whiskered form of Jesus Christ.

With my facial hair concerns negated, we pushed onward and arrived at the 373rd step. We stood, surrounded by the Ten Commandments, with our hands on our heads holding down our hats, being battered by the wind while we admired the spectacular 360-degree view.

To the east, the Colorado plains—flat, stretching away from us until they became the sky. Occupying part of them was the vast sprawl of mankind, with all the fervor of a major U.S. city. To the west, the rugged beauty and serenity of the snow-capped Rocky Mountains. Running north and south, the thin wavy dividing line of the foothills, not the massive mountains that start a few miles to the west, but enough of a rising challenge to make the early settlers look at each other and say, "This seems a good place to stop."

The continual pushing and shoving from the wind was like being bullied on a playground. Leaving appeared to be the wisest choice. The descent was quick. We passed an out-of-breath, red-faced elderly couple who were making shaky progress up the arduous ascent. I wondered what would be inscribed on their plaque.

Upon reaching the base we headed to the spring. Armed with our little paper cones, we sampled the fresh spring water, which didn't taste as fresh as I thought fresh spring water might taste. I guess I forgot that adding the holy healing element to spring water would naturally change the taste, similar to adding a slice of lemon or cucumber. I have always found that adding additional items to my water invariably spoils the taste, but I was far happier accepting this addition than the regular offerings of fruit or vegetable flavors.

I noticed a small chapel built on the side of the hill, constructed from Colorado Red Flagstone, and I was drawn to it. We walked over. The sunlight hit the front, highlighting the soft hues of the beautiful natural stone. We swung open the front doors and the three of us went in. The complete stillness was amplified by the sudden absence of the wind. The windowless room banished the bright sun. The only light came from hundreds of flickering votive candles, which had been lit by the faithful. They stood row upon row on racks, each tier a little higher than the previous. Small ordinary candles stacked in iron racks, one after the other, their parts plain, but their meaning extraordinary, deep, and loving. Each lit by someone, for somebody; celebrating a life, a dream, or a prayer. Each one specifically unique to the human soul it was attached to when the flame was ignited. Each continuing to glow steadily.

The magical light from the candles surrounded and caressed us with the soft warmth of natural flame. In hushed reverence, we surveyed our surroundings. A small altar stood in front of us adorned with simple religious artifacts and more candles. I noticed three or four other people moving slowly around the tiny chapel in measured steps, soaking in the remarkable atmosphere.

Passing the many plaques on our trip up to the shrine prompted a discussion about my mother who had passed away a short time before. Now it seemed only fitting to light a candle on her behalf. I bent down and whispered in my daughter's ear. She seemed excited at the prospect. We selected a rack near the rear of the chapel and stood in front of it, our faces softly lit by the fifty or so candles that were already burning. Maitland picked out the centrally located unlit candle she would light for Sylvia. I put a few dollars into the collection box and handed her a wooden taper. She held the tip of the taper above one of the lit candles until, with a small crackle, her taper burst to life. Then very carefully she guided the burning tip towards Sylvia's unlit candle, holding it to the waxed wick. Moments later, there was a little surge of new light.

Maitland withdrew the taper and then paused for a quiet thought and prayer. The whole process was contemplatively paced and performed with great reverence. It moved me and it seemed to affect Maitland. She then held the burning taper in front of her mouth in readiness to blow it out. She inhaled and blew a small but strong stream of air towards the tiny flame. The veracity with which she blew sent a jet stream of cold wind right through the taper, extinguishing it immediately. Surprisingly, the wind continued. Dissatisfied with the simple act of knocking out a solitary flame it swirled its way into the midst of the happy bank of religious candles. What started as an innocent puff was now an out-of-control gale, wreaking havoc as it wildly snuffed out candles indiscriminately.

Like most natural disasters, it happened too quickly to predict or avoid. One moment everything is copacetic, then in an uncontrollable instant you are left attempting to mop up and rebuild. In my estimation, a total of eight to twelve candles were gone. Eight to twelve souls, memories, prayers snatched away forever. We looked in horror at the destruction we'd caused. But what, in fact had we caused? What were the true ramifications? Was it just a memory burning there or was it something more? What if it represented the person's soul? An innocent fragile flicker holding a person's hopes and dreams as they attempted to climb the 373 steps to heaven. What if the extinguishing of that flame sent their soul tumbling down to the rocky, fiery depths of hell? Or was the flame a small window to allow the deceased a momentary glimpse back into this world, a brief view of their loved ones, which slammed shut when extinguished, isolating them in cold, icy darkness forever? What if the person who the candle represented wasn't dead at all, just sick with some terrible disease? Had we now prevented the miracle cure and doomed the patient to certain death?

The only conclusion I could draw for sure from these brief panicked thoughts was that nothing good comes from blowing out somebody else's religious candle.

Highly concerned about the current predicament and naturally quite terrified by the fact that other people may have seen us commit this grievous crime, I glanced nervously around the chapel. When extinguishing a single match, an alarming amount of smoke is created, curling up into the sky while leaving behind a pungent smell of snuffed disappointment. Multiply this by twelve and it produces nothing short of a small mushroom cloud billowing up to the chapel's rafters where it is bound to leave a mark. Not just on the ceiling but quite possibly on eternity.

The smell of the accidental snuffing alone was enough to make a person stop dead in his tracks, stand bolt upright, and shout at the top of his lungs, "Fire!" Then, the unfortunate would run wildly—because when panicked, running feels right. Running was now on the top of my list of things to do. Grab the kids and bolt. However, after completing a survey of my fellow chapel attendees, I concluded, much to my amazement, that this incident had gone unnoticed.

So here was my chance to rectify the situation, to restore a certain cosmic order. I grabbed the taper from my very wide-eyed daughter, who had obviously quickly grasped the severity of her puff, and lit it. I then started to light candles willy-nilly. I wasn't at all sure which candles had been extinguished, but thought it better to err on the side of over- rather than under-lighting. While doing this, I found myself muttering what I can only describe as my own made-up religious chant of apology, while attempting to incorporate as many random names as possible in the hopeful, but statistically unlikely, event that I'd hit upon some winners and match some candles with the correct original names, thus restoring some form of eternal harmony.

Soon the rows of votive candles were returned to their former glory. The three of us stood before them relieved, my mildly perspiring face surrounded once again by their natural glow. Of course it was impossible for me not to wonder what the true value of a relit candle was. Were they now just candles burning as candles burn or did they have the ability to remember their previous purpose? Once reignited are they able, like a homing pigeon, to doggedly seek out their original destination? I hoped and prayed for it to be so.

We exited the chapel and were blown to the minivan. Moments later we wound down the steep road, away from the Mother Cabrini Shrine, our outing complete. During the drive home, I sent up one last prayer of apology in an attempt to ease my conscience, "Dear To Whom it May Concern, If your soul has indeed plummeted to the deep dark depth of purgatory, condemning you to an eternity of fire and brimstone, all because of the careless breath of my child's lips, I'm really, really sorry … Amen."

20
CAN YOU HEAR ME?

I HAD NEVER BEFORE KNOWN someone in a coma. Not only did I *know* Art, he was my best friend. He had fallen more than twenty-five feet while on a construction site and hit his head.

We all gathered at St. Mary's Hospital in Grand Junction, Colorado. I stood anxiously in a small waiting room with Art's family and friends. I had driven from Denver in the wee hours of the morning after the distance between Art and me had become too much to bear. The waiting room decorator had decided the occupants of this room would have too much on their minds to want to deal with bold and unusual decorative choices. The result: a world that was square and beige, all very comfortable and safe; the exact opposite of the room's current occupants.

Several people, including Art's sixteen-year-old daughter Mackenzie, were well into their second day at the hospital, worry and fatigue etched into their tired faces. We milled around in the room waiting for news from the doctors. It was hard for me to just sit. As soon as I had settled into the comfortably dull furniture, I found it impossible to relax. I circled the room like a goldfish trapped in a bowl, waiting for a doctor to crumble some more flakes of information my way. Pockets of people gathered, swapping stories or just listening, occasionally offering to run errands; all of us desperately trying to navigate the same troubled waters. The kindness people show to each other in times of great hardship is a beautiful testament to the fact that human beings are inherently good.

When the doctor did arrive with an update, we all congregated around his white lab coat, clipboard, and silvery-grey hair, and listened intently. He presented his report in a clear, even tone. He kept the content understandable while sprinkling in enough medical terminology to inhibit us from questioning his abilities.

"... weaken the synaptic functioning ..."

"... inconclusive ..."

"... apparent Hypoxia ..."

He showed warmth and concern, and once he had delivered this chapter of his somber tale he patiently answered our questions as we tried to pry from him a glimmer of hope. Our doctor sailed the narrow passage between Art's life and death. He skillfully communicated the medical facts, yet he tendered a little hope for us to cling to, while being careful not to create a false sense of optimism.

What an amazing job he had. Through dedication, hard work, and years of study, he now possessed the skills to save lives, but that wasn't enough. He was also expected to care for the perfectly healthy but terrified family and friends of the sick. I often hear about the shortcomings of the American healthcare system, but I have to remember its failings rarely lie at the feet of the hundreds of thousands of dedicated doctors and nurses who provide the care.

Periodically, people were allowed to visit Art in his room. I waited patiently for my turn, trying to be considerate, but I desperately wanted to be with him. I was finally offered my chance to visit. Immediately, I began to doubt myself. I didn't know what to expect, what to say, or how to behave. Luckily, Sally, a dear family friend of Art's, agreed to accompany me, and as we set off through the glass double doors I tried to compose myself, thankful for Sally's positive and effervescent spirit.

We stopped at the nurse's station and washed our hands, then Sally led me in. I walked through the door and into a profound quiet—as if I had just entered a church occupied by a single prayerful parishioner. I thought to myself, *Be quiet Matthew, you don't want to wake him.* There Art lay, serene and peaceful. Remarkably unmarked, considering the fall he had taken.

I stood a few feet inside the room and observed Sally as she gently talked to him with soft, tender words. He lay propped up in his bed—broad-chested, his strong arms and thick hands to each side. His powerful legs emerged where his hospital gown ended, stretching the length of the bed. He seemed ready to ride or ski, as soon as his brain was once again in command. He looked proud and defiant in this externally peaceful yet life-threatening slumber.

As I looked at him, I thought about what a great friend he was and how much his friendship meant to me. I wished I had told him this during the last brief visit we had together while building my fence in the spring. I wished I had expressed my feelings before the opportunity had been unexpectedly snatched away.

In my initial minutes of being in the room, I had only noticed Art. It was quite a while before I became aware of what was attached to Art. He was hooked up to everything modern science had to offer. The dim room was in part lit by the ghostly green lights from an array of medical equipment displaying a digital depiction of Art's fragile existence. A mass of tubes and wires ran between him and the bank of blinking lights that helped the doctors monitor Art's inner struggle. Another machine helped Art breathe, buying precious time in the hope that he could beat the odds and return to us.

I moved closer. I touched his hand. It was warm, living, and it gave me an instant spark of hope. "Well, this is a fine mess you've gotten yourself into. You're scaring the shit out of me!" I didn't mean to scold him, but the words just burst out. I confess, it felt great. I continued with my mild tongue lashing. Sally laughed through her tears at the utter inappropriateness of the whole situation. After my initial reprimand, I continued sharing thoughts and memories, laughing and crying. Sally and I encouraged him to fight, although I knew Art needed no encouragement—he had too many wonderful things in his life to live for and was never one to slip quietly away from a challenge.

After about ten minutes, a nurse came in and explained that according to the myriad of machines, Art was getting a tad bit too excited and we should bring our visit to a close. The overly-stimulated Art lay there motionless, except for the steady mechanically-aided breaths easing in and out of his large lungs that caused his chest to rise and then fall. His calm face and softly shut eyes gave the impression of a deep, peaceful slumber. The machines told a very different story—the story of Art's brain and its hyperactivity. It was impossible not to notice the ever-changing data displayed in wavy lines and numbers on the many monitors surrounding him. The doctors were patient and helpful in deciphering the complex information for us laymen. The one thing they could not explain was what Art was actually experiencing.

Was the excessive neural activity due to the fact that he was engaged in a massive and brutal battle for his very existence as he clung desperately to the thin shreds of his life? I imagined him hanging above a black abyss, stubbornly refusing to let go—refusing to be swallowed by the silent darkness. Or perhaps he could hear every word we said as clear as a bell, which would account for the immense effort he was exerting as he attempted to communicate one last time. I pictured Mackenzie standing next to him, and I thought of Art's insatiable need to reach out and touch her face, gently pushing her hair to one side and confidently telling her how much he loved her and how, in time, it would all be okay.

How unfair and cruel it would be to have your last words stolen from you.

I looked at his face and again touched his warm hand with mine. I hoped that through this physical contact a connection could be made. I shut my eyes and listened with all my might. *Tell me something Art. Can you hear me? Are you there?* I had to hear something. Something I could pass on to Mackenzie, something for all of us in this world who knew him. Some words of encouragement, hope, and comfort. Nothing came. But those numbers kept increasing. Art was getting worked up. It was time to go.

So with a soft squeeze of his hand, I left. As I walked out the doorway, I turned for what would prove to be my last look at my dear friend Art. I whispered a soft good-bye, which I needed to believe he heard.

21
THANK YOU, SIR

I LOOKED UP at the living room clock to confirm I was on schedule—10:40 a.m. Perfect. I worked for another three minutes, glanced up again, and was flabbergasted to see that the clock now read 10:56. I was officially late. Instructors at Denver's elite Colorado Athletic Club are never late. I grabbed my bag and flew out the back door. My stomach sank at the sight of the empty driveway. My wife had taken the car, leaving me with only one option: *Scooter Power*.

The words *scooter* and *power* are rarely used together and for good reason—it's a lie. My scooter's total engine capacity is less than 50cc. Engines under 50cc are usually found powering household appliances. Even with my slender frame perched atop the scooter, she still struggles to surpass twenty-eight miles per hour. (And that's downhill with a tailwind.)

The humbling limitation of riding the bottom rung of the cc ladder still cannot lessen the love I have for my scooter. I marvel at how she always brings a smile to my face. A smile most people can easily focus on as I ride by at an agonizingly slow pace. If there is a need for speed, there most certainly isn't a need for a scooter. But on this particular day the scooter would have to do.

I opened the garage, put on my helmet, then wheeled out the crimson and cream beast. One aggressive stomp of her kick-start brought Sylvia roaring to life. I jumped on board and gave the throttle a sharp twist. The engine labored but created no forward motion. Two quick pushes with my feet was all the help the feeble engine needed. We were off tooling down 32nd Avenue towards downtown, just three miles away.

Few things in the world are as simple as riding a scooter. Get on, open up the throttle, and go. Repeat as necessary. No wonder I smile so much—it is just that easy.

I was making good time as I approached downtown, confident of beating my students to the class. I slowed to make a left turn onto Stout Street and noticed a motorcycle cop parked threateningly on the median, ready to leap into action. I chuckled to myself, yet another reason to smile. It is a physical impossibility to get a speeding ticket on Sylvia. I zipped along 14th Street by the convention center and headed towards Welton Street where the health club awaited me three blocks to the north.

A quick glance in my side mirror revealed a shock. There, riding behind me was the motorcycle cop. *Why is he behind me? Nobody is ever behind me.* The traffic light turned red, and the cop drew up next to me on his 1200cc Harley Davidson, vibrating with power. To my surprise, he signaled for me to pull over to the side of the road. For a split second I had the urge to gun it—to take the cop by surprise and rely on my superior maneuverability and handling skills to lose him in the busy downtown traffic. I envisioned an exciting James Bond-style chase scene winding through the streets of Denver—down back alleys and along busy sidewalks. Pedestrians would scatter as I plowed through a hot dog vendor's wagon, upset a large fruit stand, and careened down the steps of City Hall, knocking over six trash cans at the bottom. Eventually, Sylvia and I would emerge victorious as we puttered off nonchalantly into the sunset, offering a cheeky wave to an angry and befuddled police officer shaking his fist in my wake, the twisted metal of his motorcycle still smoking.

But that would be breaking the law.

I dutifully obliged and headed to the curb, still stunned that I was being pulled over. I was not the only person who appeared surprised—a large percentage of the convention attendees, whom I would have been scattering in all directions had I gone for it, seemed to be taking interest in the curious scene unfolding before them. A sea of light blue dress shirts and khaki pants converged on me, each batting at their oversized name tag lanyards caught unexpectedly in the downtown breeze. I reluctantly parked Sylvia, accepting that I would now be late for my own class, and removed my helmet. The police officer eased his Harley to the side of the curb in front of me, cutting off the escape as if he had been anticipating my James Bond fantasy. He dismounted smoothly with the familiarity that only comes with years of practice. A turn of the key silenced the Hog. Fixated on his prey, he swaggered towards me. I looked directly back at his Ray-Ban Aviator sunglasses. I was suddenly very impressed by the realism of the TV show C.Hi.P.S.

The entire scene was rather disproportionate. There stood Sylvia—a sprightly Venice Twist and Go 49.8cc scooter, her fetching crimson-and-cream color scheme accentuating her smooth and graceful lines. She is perky, pretty in the sun, and ready to join the scooter sorority as soon as the other girls get their act together. Looming in front of her was the police officer's motorcycle. I didn't ask the name of his bike, but I'm sure it was Thor. Thor was 1200cc's of brute force. All black and blue with police decals, colored lights, and chrome. He gleamed coolly at Sylvia. If Thor wasn't on duty, he would be in a blue-collar sports bar drinking Pabst Blue Ribbon and eating insanely hot buffalo wings without flinching. To match the colossal power of Thor, I imagined twenty-four Sylvias lined up next to each other, all with their front wheels cocked at a cute forty-five-degree angle.

The police officer towered before me. His perfectly pressed extra-extra-large blue uniform shirt was short-sleeved. It would always have to be, since no long-sleeved shirt would be capable of accommodating his bulging, iron-pumped biceps and forearms, which hung loosely at his sides allowing his hands to be near, but not threateningly near, his holstered firearm. The sleeves flaunted two upside-down chevrons that indicated to me this was not his first day on the job. His broad shoulders provided ample surface area for the various ribbons and badges attached to his sprawling epaulettes. His chest pushed out towards me, tempting me to poke it. Lower down, his stomach continued out in a soft, rounded curve until it met his thick black belt. His belly added additional mass that augmented his obvious immense strength.

His uniform pants had that Jodhpur look, although I doubted he'd ever been on the back of a horse. They tucked neatly into his highly polished, knee-length motorcycle boots with leather soles and a considerable heel, possible insurance that he would always look down upon the lawbreakers of the world. His strong jaw and stern face squeezed out of his rigid helmet, which added an inch-and-a-half to his already impressive height. To match the colossal power of the officer, I imagined twenty-four Matthews lined up neatly next to each other, all with our heads cocked at a cute forty-five-degree angle. It was obvious—if I didn't cooperate I would get my ass kicked by Thor's bitch.

The officer spoke for the first time. His voice sounded as if he had been snacking on a bag of gravel.

"May I see your license and registration, please?"

"Yes, Sir," I replied, instantly jumping to attention. *"Yes, Sir?" What's up with that?* The chance that this behemoth of a policeman had been knighted by Queen Elizabeth II was slim to none. I think it was a safe bet that Thor's bitch wasn't truly a "Sir." But at this moment in time, whether the authority figure in front of me was legitimately titled or not made no difference. I "sir-ed" him left, right, and center, as if I'd suddenly enlisted in the Queen's Guards.

"This is your insurance, not your registration."

"Yes, Sir."

"I don't need to see your insurance."

"Really, Sir?"

"I do need to see your registration."

"Oh, Sir."

"Do you have registration?"

"No, Sir."

He strolled the short distance back to his bike and took out a metal clipboard. Clipped to the board was that horrible yellow paper signaling that bad news was imminent.

He told me where I had to go to get Sylvia registered. He seemed happy to explain that it would only cost me five dollars and seventy-five cents for three years. I leaned in to see what he was writing and thought, *If registration is only five dollars and seventy-five cents for three years, how the bloody hell can my ticket be for the ridiculous amount of $105?! That's over fifty years' worth of registration fees! This is a load of bullocks!* What I actually said to him was, "$105—sir?" As a response, he blathered on about scooter etiquette, safety rules, and regulations. I felt the $105 bleed out of my wallet.

When he was good and ready and I had been sufficiently schooled, he handed me the flimsy yellow ticket. As if he'd given me a present, I impulsively responded, "Thank you … Sir."

... You're listening to The Style Slander on
KBUT 90.3 FM in Crested Butte, Colorado ...

IN THE FALL OF 1985, six months after leaving my
homeland of England, I stumbled into the small mountain town of Crested Butte, Colorado. I fell in love with
the town and decided to linger ... for five years. I still
marvel at the myriad of opportunities presented to me
due simply to the fact that I chose to live in a small American town.

The enormous land mass that constitutes the United
States of America creates vast distances between population centers. By contrast, cities, towns, and villages in
England are packed closely together and are easily served
by single centralized services. Radio is a prime example. I
grew up listening to Radio One on the British Broadcast-

ing Corporation. There was also BBC Two, BBC Three, and BBC Four. All were available, depending upon your tastes, and to a certain degree, your age. Because of the BBC's dominance of the airwaves, the number of small, independent stations was limited. Consequently, in England the chances of becoming a DJ were miniscule. Imagine my surprise, when, in December 1986, Crested Butte (population 997) started its own radio station and a notice was sent out inviting everyone to audition for the position of DJ. The process was not arduous—all you needed to do was be able to say the words, "Yes, I would like to be a DJ."

A week later, my good friend Art and I were put through a rigorous two-hour training program and, upon completion, were given the prestigious title of Crested Butte Disc Jockeys. They gave us a week to come up with the style and format for our show. During our training session, they encouraged us to find songs that would transition nicely into each other.

"Before your show," they instructed, "listen to the ends and beginnings of your songs so you can create a smooth, well-orchestrated playlist."

This made sense to us aesthetically, but unfortunately it also sounded like work. Not something we'd signed up for. Now please, don't get me wrong—we wanted to be and were excited to be DJ's, but it just wasn't critical to us that we be *good* DJ's.

With this work ethic firmly in place, we had to come up with the name for our show. We knew we were novices, so rather than simply look bad when song after song didn't fit well together, we hoped that if we called our show *The Style Slander* people would think we'd done it on purpose. To help our listeners understand that the jarring transitions were skillfully planned, we started each show by playing "Sex and Drugs and Rock n' Roll" by Ian Jury and the Blockheads, followed by "These are a Few of My Favorite Things" by Julie Andrews from *The Sound of Music.*

The Style Slander aired on Thursday nights from 10:00 p.m. to midnight. When you are having fun time flies, and two hours never seemed like enough. A benefit of being the last show of the night was that the station manager, Jim Michaels, gave us the option to continue into the wee hours if we so desired, as long as we promised to behave and lock up. However, this presented a problem. Without a concrete ending time, we often found ourselves still on the air at 6:00 a.m. on Friday morning, which destroyed any chance of productivity for the rest of the day, whether that was skiing, mountain biking, or heavens forbid, real work. We had to come up with a plan that would prevent the show from lasting until sunrise.

To this day I am proud of the simple, efficient, and creative plan we adopted. *The KBUT Style Slander* radio show would officially last the length of time it took two devoted DJs to consume a fifteen-pack of Stroh's beer. To my knowledge, there is no other radio show whose duration has been governed exclusively by thirst.

So here's how it worked: a few minutes before 10:00 p.m., we arrived armed with our fifteen-pack. We then queued up Ian Dury, cracked a beer, and dropped the needle. If friends visited us at the station, or we were just plain thirsty, the show was shortened. If we were in a quieter reflective mood, the show might run long. Regardless of which way it went, we had a definitive ending time. As soon as the last drop of beer left the last can, the show abruptly ended. No fuss, no words, no clever farewells. Just the scratch of the needle roughly removed from the vinyl, followed by a silence that always took *both* of our listeners by surprise.

Although we never worried about our jarring transitions, we did pay attention to the general theme from week to week. Like the show where we played two Elton John tunes in a row and enjoyed it so much that we played a third and then a fourth. Three-and-a-half hours later, we had played every Elton John song ever written. Or *The Style Slander's Mid-Winter Summer Vacation Show*, which aired in February. Every song had a light, warm summery theme. So inspired by our premise, our dear friend Bookie arrived unannounced at the station. She was fully decked in her summer floral dress, giant hat, and armed with a strawberry shortcake. At the end of that show (a bit after four in the morning), we all spontaneously drove straight from the radio station 687 miles to Phoenix, Arizona to worship the sun in person.

Then there was *The Style Slander's Major Motown Show*. This came about when Tom Lucci, manager of the Grub Steak restaurant, told us that a friend of his in Detroit had sent a cassette tape of classic and obscure Motown songs. Art and I were eleven cans into the show when we played the first track off Tom's cassette. As the song drew to a close, I readied myself with an album on one of the turntables. I was just about to start the record when to my surprise the song on the cassette tape seamlessly faded into another song. I had no choice at that point but to let it run. This proved to be a brilliant decision, since the new song was excellent. Once again I prepared for the end of the second song on the tape. My fingers hovered above the turntable only to have the same exact thing happen again.

Art and I looked at each other and grinned. DJ's never get to experience their show the same way their listeners do, yet here was our chance. It would be foolish to squander the opportunity. We wasted no time. We grabbed our coats, our remaining cans of Stroh's, and raced down the narrow stairs out into the frozen parking lot. We jumped into Art's Ford Fairlane. A twist of the key awoke the slumbering giant. A green light glowed from the middle of the dash. I tuned the radio dial to 90.3 FM. Into the chilly winter night floated the warm sounds of *The Style Slander*. I looked at Art with a devilish grin spreading across my face and said, "Come on Art, you know we can do this. Let's drive."

A sharp yank on the gear shift produced a dull clunk from the transmission. The Ford Fairlane slowly pulled away from KBUT, separating us from our show. We cruised slowly around the block, knowing that if anything happened we could dash back to the station in a flash. It felt odd being connected to the music yet strangely detached at the same time. It reminded me of a time I sat at an isolated table in the Chichester College library taking an economics exam that I hadn't studied for. My fellow students violently scribbled away while I sat knowing that I was in the right place but feeling oddly distant due to my blank paper and mind.

The third song drew to a close. I looked anxiously at Art. We held our breath, bracing ourselves for the dreaded extended silence that is the trademark of crappy DJ's.

"Awesome!" shouted Art as another fabulous Motown classic flooded the airways.

With growing confidence I added, "Man, this tape makes us sound really good." I was beginning to feel amazingly comfortable in my new role as listener of *The Style Slander*.

As our confidence grew, we ventured further afield. We turned right on Crested Butte's main street, Elk Avenue. Another song ended, another song started. Without discussion, we drew up outside the Wooden Nickel Bar. It was 1:35 a.m. Ed, the bartender, was clearly visible through the large window. He stood behind the bar, serving patrons their final libations. He glanced up and saw us climbing out of Art's car. He was perplexed as he looked up at the speakers hanging over his bar and then pointed back at us. We entered and were greeted by the dulcet tones of *The Style Slander*. We sat at the bar, ordered a couple of beers and listened. Ed returned with our drinks and slyly said, "You guys make being disc jockeys look really easy."

"Thank you," we said in unison. We were in complete agreement. Every time a song came to an end, Art and I glanced at each other with a mischievous glint in our eyes, ready for a mad dash to the car. Then, we smiled as our show effortlessly continued.

After twenty-five minutes, "I Heard it Through the Grapevine" by Marvin Gaye eased its way through the sound system. This was met with great approval by the remaining patrons at the bar. This longer song presented us with the perfect opportunity to return to the station. Plus, we realized a classic like this could easily be the end of the tape. We jumped in the car and drove hell-for-leather back to the station. The song was winding down as I bounded three steps at a time up the stairway. I flung open the studio door and there, cued up on the turntable, was the record I had placed forty minutes earlier. Marvin Gaye sang his last notes and without a second to spare, I triumphantly pushed "play" on turntable B and faded it up artfully. We had made it. My self-congratulatory smile slowly faded from my lips as the studio speakers put forth the unmistakable opening bars of that Motown classic, "I Heard it Through the Grapevine."

23
SOUTHERN EXPOSURE

THE PHONE RANG AGAIN as it had incessantly all day. It appeared that everybody on the south coast of England deemed it necessary to purchase a house today. I answered it, struggling to maintain my chipper countenance. "Jackson-Stops and Staff, this is Matthew." The chatty cadence of the caller hinted to me that she had all the time in the world and was oblivious to the fact that I did not. I had an important field hockey league match to play in fifty minutes.

While on the phone, Mike Hole, my ride to the game, drew up in front of the estate agency and deftly reversed his mini into a postage-stamp-sized parking space. He glanced through the office windows between the elegantly displayed pictures of opulent West Sussex properties, saw me on the phone behind my desk, and waved. I felt compelled to communicate. I offered an overly complicated hand gesture. Mike smiled the kind of smile you smile when you have no idea what the other person is attempting to communicate.

All I had to do was end my call, grab my hockey bag, and dash to the car. Three-quarters of the way out of my chair, I straightened my desk with my free hand and tried every trick in the book to ease myself out of the conversation.

"Let me check into that and get back to you tomorrow—"

"I've got another call on the other—"

I even feigned that another person had entered my office saying breezily to no one, "Yes, I'll be right with you, Mr. Jenkins."

All to no avail.

Mike's patience was running thin. His hand gesture was much clearer than mine had been. *Put down the bloody phone and get in the car. NOW!*

The chances of us making it to the game on time were now becoming slim. Try as I might, I just couldn't get off the phone. Suddenly, Mike hit the limits of his gesticulation. He slammed his hand hard down on the horn of the mini. You would think Austin Morris would have had the decency to equip a mini with a proportionally louder horn in comparison to the size of the vehicle. Then the car, when confronted with an altercation, could at least puff up its feathers and flex its muscles through its horn's volume, even if its size was still something to be mocked. Instead, my phone conversation was now being punctuated by what sounded like the horn from an angry clown car.

At last, I managed with only a modicum of rudeness to extricate myself from Miss Limpet. I hung up, grabbed my bag, and rushed outside. A frustrated Mike Hole said, "Come on, Taylor, we need to fly or we'll miss the start of the game." Mike was a short, wiry man with a buzz cut. He always looked healthy, happy, and fit. He played hockey in a relentlessly energetic and efficient way, which was also how he conducted his life. He reminded me of a Jack Russell Terrier. Small, muscular, busy—but Mike never snarled. He smiled and laughed instead.

I threw my bag onto the rear seat and squeezed into the car. Seconds later, we drew into the busy traffic on South Street and headed out of Chichester towards the Donnington Roundabout.

The game was in Portsmouth, some thirty-five miles to the west, so we would have to take the A-27 along the South Coast. Parts of the road had been improved and were now dual carriageways. However, large sections were still single lane and created horrible bottlenecks. The traffic was heavy. In a desperate attempt to pick up time, Mike dodged frenetically in and out of traffic lanes until we were forced to a complete standstill just outside Emsworth. We sat flustered in bumper-to-bumper traffic.

I felt my guilt building as I realized I had let Mike, as well as the entire team, down. I had to suggest something. We just couldn't sit here. I owed it to my teammates. "Inland!" I barked. "Let's do it!" yelled Mike with his game face on.

"Go," I said, pointing to a gap in the oncoming traffic. He peeled across the road and zoomed up a small side street. Skillfully, he maneuvered the mini through the streets of Emsworth, heading inland. The traffic eased. Our goal was to connect with a small windy country road eight miles inland that ran parallel to the coast. It was our only hope.

At last we joined with the A-23. Mike pointed the mini west and depressed the accelerator to the floor. We were off in a mad sprint to the game, winding our way left and right, up and down through the rolling farmland of the South Downs. It was like being on a rollercoaster ride. *This just might work, but it will be close.* Mike looked at his watch, then at me, and said with a serious tone, "You need to change into your hockey kit." At this rate, we would be screeching in right as the game started. Mike was already in his hockey gear, but I was still in my business suit. He was right. I needed to change en route.

Minis are aptly named vehicles. If a car was manufactured any smaller than a mini, it would be called a toy. Everything is small—the wheels, the windows, the engine. The interior is also to scale with little baby seats, a tiny steering wheel, and a *glove* compartment that is honest—only capable of holding one of your two gloves.

With two full-grown men wedged up front, the prospect of changing wasn't pretty. We lurched back and forth. I gingerly released my seatbelt and uneasily removed my tie. Curling forward into a hunch, I pulled my suit jacket up and over my head and wriggled my arms out. Every now and then, I could feel Mike's hand pushing my arm away as it obscured his view. I freed one of my arms, allowing me to look up and out of the windscreen inches from my nose. The lane swung from right to left and shot under the car as we careened forward. I released my other arm, threw the jacket into the back, then unbuttoned and removed my shirt, revealing to the world my skinny upper body. I reached for my belt, unbuckled it, and in one fluid motion unzipped my trousers. A breeze rushed in as if filling a vacuum.

I realized this reluctant striptease would soon leave me completely naked in a mini next to another man while barreling down a country road at fifty mph. I compromised. I would settle on half-naked at a time. Leaning over to the backseat, I grabbed my Havant Hockey Club sweatshirt. I slipped it on and was instantly comforted by the coverage.

Now I was able to focus on the more sensitive bottom half. Every now and then, Mike braked hard to stop at a crossroads, check both ways, and then shoot forward at full speed. Bracing my head against the dashboard, I stretched down and slipped off my shoes. I tugged at my socks, separating them from my feet. The car lurched to the right, forcing my cheek to momentarily touch Mike's thigh. "Bloody hell, Taylor," he grunted as he elbowed my ear. I eased back up. This was far more stretching than I would ever normally do before a game. I started to bounce up and down in the seat to wiggle off my trousers. I struggled to get them down my legs and over my bare feet. I sighed, pushed my feet against the floorboard, and tensed my leg muscles to lift myself an inch off the seat. I grabbed at the elastic of my underwear and swiftly yanked off my boxers.

I relaxed and dropped back down onto the front seat. My eyes opened wide as my bare buttocks greeted the vinyl. I grabbed my jockstrap, excited at the prospect of adding clothes to my totally naked bottom half. The car braked violently, throwing me against the windscreen, the pressure pinning me to the glass. My body became so heavy I was unable to move. I sensed the onset of pain mixed with confusion and fear. I heard the screech of tires, then a loud crunch accompanied by the sounds of crumpling metal and shattering glass. The release tossed me like a rag doll back into my seat. Mike had rear-ended the car in front of us. A stunned silence followed. My brain took inventory quickly. *Am I alive? Yes. Is Mike alive? Yes. Am I naked? Yes.*

The gentleman we crashed into was also very much alive. I knew this because he was already out of his car. His dark suit, dull tie, and neatly cut, thinning grey hair made me feel like we were about to be audited. I would never wish anyone harm from an accident, but I wouldn't have minded if he'd received a minor leg wound—just enough to keep him in his car. No such luck. He stormed towards us looking shocked and concerned. Still limply holding my jockstrap in my hand, I couldn't help thinking his shock and concern was about to heighten. Fortunately he was heading to the driver's side, and Mike had recovered enough to be able to talk. Hopefully, I wouldn't have to play a major role in the confrontation.

I busied myself with a new experiment: What is the maximum stretchability of a Havant Hockey Club sweatshirt? I grabbed the bottom and yanked it down with all my might to maximize my meager coverage. With the stranger just a few feet from the car and my sweatshirt three times its regular size, I ceased the stretching.

I assumed a nonchalant pose. To avoid eye contact, I gazed out the side window with my head tilted slightly and my whole body angled away from the stranger. My sweatshirt cut into the back of my neck and created a plunging neckline to the front, which stopped an inch above my chilled nipples. I looked like a naked man wearing a sweatshirt.

Mike rolled down his window and beat the stranger to the punch, "Sorry, my fault, couldn't stop in time, are you all right?"

"Yes, I'm a little shaken but fine. How about you?" replied the man, visibly relieved that Mike was accepting full responsibility and showing no hostility.

They chatted briefly. Had it turned ugly, I wouldn't have been a very good backup. I added nothing. During the conversation I stared transfixed out the side window of the car towards the field, much like a child witnessing for the first time livestock copulating. Mike got out, and they both came round to the front of the mini to inspect the minimal damage. I sat there feeling like the star in a peepshow. Insurance information was exchanged. Mike returned to the car, and we were on our way. We didn't speak. I finished changing amidst the somber silence. We arrived late for the game.

Being male is sometimes hard. We communicate less openly than females and occasionally leave nagging questions unanswered. Did the poor unsuspecting stranger ever know how naked I was? It certainly was the quickest resolve of an accident I had ever witnessed. And what caused the accident? At the moment of my most extreme nakedness … Mike smashed into the back of another car.

24
HAPPY HOUR

WE ALWAYS SIT IN THE BACK of the church. Not because I am afraid the priest will ask me a question during his homily, although I have to admit when he does on occasion ask a question of a nearby parishioner I invariably squirm—clueless as to the answer and relieved to be in my far-off pew.

My family and I sit at the back of the church because we are always late. I blame my children. They blame me. My wife blames me and the children. If I took some responsibility rather than just blaming, perhaps one day my family would sit near the middle of the church.

One such Sunday, I hushed Alastair and Maitland as we tiptoed through the side door of Saint Elizabeth's about ten minutes into the service. We settled into our distant, safe, and familiar pew, having caused minimal disturbance. I focused on the remainder of the first reading, thankful that the mad rush to church was over. I forced myself to take deep, calming breaths.

Time passed quickly, although my children would disagree. Soon it was time to celebrate the Eucharist. Our location dictated that we would be one of the last families in the church to receive the Body and Blood of Christ. As we reverently lined up for communion, I noticed my nine-year-old son Alastair allowing the few parishioners behind us to go past him until he was the last person in line.

I felt proud that Alastair delighted in exhibiting excellent manners, even more so when I remembered having seen the same scenario unfold the previous week. I shuffled up the center aisle towards the priest. Our eyes met. He held up the bread and said in an ecclesiastical tone, "The Body of Christ." He placed the bread in my crossed hands as I uttered a quiet "Amen" and ate it. Off to the side a Eucharistic minister presented me with the cup and said, "The Blood of Christ." I murmured "Amen" and took a tiny sip. I soberly returned to my seat, knelt, and prayed.

I sensed Alistair returning to the pew and kneeling dutifully next to me. A couple of minutes later, we both sat up. During the church announcements that followed I leant over to my son and whispered in his ear, "Ali, that was nice of you to let everybody go in front of you at communion." Confidently he said, "That's okay, Dad, I just like finishing up the wine."

The middle of the church has never looked better.

25
LOADED

MY FAMILY AND I ARE LUCKY to live in a well-built 1928 Craftsman bungalow in a popular up-and-coming neighborhood near downtown Denver called The Highlands. Five blocks to the east of my home is a small commercial district with hip stores, trendy restaurants, and coffee shops. The feel is as close to living in a village as I can experience in a city. People are constantly walking through the "hood" accompanied by dogs, strollers, or both. All greet each other with cheery waves and smiles. It's a happy place where the residents appreciate community and hold important such things as children, animals, health, and the environment. Our modest home sits on one of the main thoroughfares, so we are in the thick of the action. While working on our small garden, a large quantity of our time is spent greeting or being greeted.

As much as this all sounds very pleasant, it was ultimately the combination of the house and the much-loved neighborhood that led to my slow, downward spiral into depravity. I sank into the darkest depths of the human psyche and became so cold and calculating that to kill was not just an option, but an imperative.

Craftsman bungalows, with their low-pitched gabled roofs, exposed rafter tails under wide over-hanging eaves, decorative brackets, and incised perches, are beautiful to look at both inside and out. They were built in an era when there was great pride in workmanship and in the materials used. The woodwork is often what makes these bungalows stand out, because the builders sought to highlight each home's individuality with intricate details over which they labored with miters and chisels. The result: each house has its own unique nooks and crannies that break up the straight lines so commonly seen in modern construction.

When my sister Jessica and her husband Don visited us from the real Highlands of Scotland, they loved our neighborhood. Upon awakening the first morning of their visit, we congregated in the living room. Still in our pajamas, we sipped hot coffee and chatted away as the bright sunshine streamed in through the east windows, striking the hardwood floor, making it glow with a deep richness. Still slightly jetlagged, peering over her cup of coffee, her ginger hair half-kempt, Jessica said, "I can't believe you live in a city. It's so peaceful and quiet. I woke up to the gentle cooing of birds. It was like waking up in a bloody Disney movie."

When Jessica said, "… the gentle cooing of birds," I felt the left side of my face twitch uncontrollably. Not the sort of twitch that is noticeable to everybody, just the slight flutter of an eyelid, a small tilt of the head, and tightening in the neck. It was mild, something that would easily be overlooked by a therapist, but inside my head the distress signal sounded loud and clear. Sirens wailed, lights flashed wildly, bells tolled—the worried mothers of my mind grabbed their children and scurried to safety.

Most people have something in their lives that triggers an immediate, uncontrolled response, good or bad. A family member, a sports team, a school, an event, a song, a taste, a smell. A stimulus that awakens a dormant sensation and transports you back to a moment in your past so vivid it's as if you were experiencing it for the very first time. For me, it's the cooing of birds. Not any birds, mind you, but the cooing of a particular species of bird: pigeons.

I have a pigeon problem, thanks to the endless hours the skilled craftsmen spent in 1928 unintentionally creating perches and perfect nesting spots all over the exterior of my house. The pigeons are extremely appreciative, and to this day, over eighty years later, make it a point to utilize every one of them.

When I first moved into my house, I found the cooing delightful. As I became more familiar with my feathery tenants, the sound began to grate on me. Eventually the cooing became unbearable, a constant reminder of the endless buildup of pigeon poop that was slowly encasing my home.

The pigeon (also affectionately known as the rat of the skies) is unusually happy surrounding itself with its own excrement. Their poorly built nests are basically stuck together with it, like a household adhesive. When Mom and Dad Pigeon are finally blessed with a hatchling, they blissfully continue to poop in the nest as one happy family until their waste overflows, oozing and dripping upon everything beneath them.

Below the most popular perches and nests, mounds of grey and white streaked matter accumulate; smears of feces appear down walls and windows. The dark tiled roof breaks out in white splotches and blotches as it becomes infected with Pigeonitis. Temperatures rise through the late spring and early summer, drying the ever-growing mounds of fecal matter, which then release a uniquely pungent scent that lingers lazily on the soft summer breeze. Having experienced the species on such an intimate level, I now understand why they don't release pigeons at the opening of the Olympic Games. It is also clearer to me why the lyricist of "The Twelve Days of Christmas," after swans, geese, calling birds, French hens, turtle doves, and a partridge, had to break the avian motif and remove the *five pigeons pooing* in favor of some unrelated gold rings.

I have always had a love of nature and animals, but this pigeon menace was too much to bear. I knew I had to remove them from my house. Over the next few years, I tried every trick on the Internet. I put up a wooden owl, whom the pigeons happily befriended. I installed spikes, put out sticky paper and carpet gripper strips, wired off areas, boarded up areas, acquired cats, shouted and clapped, all to no avail. When I hear people talk about homing pigeons, I never realized they meant *my* home. Every time a new anti-pigeon method failed, my frustration and desperation grew.

Talk of pigeons dominated my conversation. "So sorry to hear about the death of your grandmother, but how much arsenic do you think it might take to kill a pigeon?" I constantly sought advice. Was there something out there I'd not tried? I didn't realize how desperate I was until I found myself deep in a conversation with a stranger in the grocery line discussing the merits of firearms. The faint hint of a sadistic smile fluttered across my face as I imagined a grey feathered target in the crosshairs of a semi-automatic weapon.

I have never been a hunter. That gene missed me, evidenced by the fact that I cried while watching Bambi ... as an adult. The idea of taking the life of any living creature, even for food, doesn't sit well with me. The thrill of the kill would never be thrilling enough to outweigh the remorse I would feel remembering a large pair of helpless, soft-brown doe eyes looking directly at me as she happily said what were to be her last words to her family, "Look kids! That man's pointing at me."

I have friends who hunt, and they are quick to remind me that they use every bit of the animal, that nothing is left to waste. They only kill what they can use. I'm a little skeptical about this claim, since I've never heard any of them say things like, "On your way out, be sure to take another bottle of our homemade glue," or "Anyone for another hoof?" I prefer to see wildlife wild and with life.

This conviction changed dramatically one hot summer day when I went outside my house and found my two young children playing in the garden. Not with a ball or a stick, but with a pile of pigeon poop. It was everywhere, covering my darling children from head to toe. My primal instincts surfaced as my anger rose like a basilisk in a Harry Potter movie. Suddenly, all pigeons were a direct threat to my young. It was us or them. And I knew it wasn't going to be us. I calmly and deliberately walked into the house, found the small crumpled piece of paper with the number on it that I thought I would never need, picked up the phone, and called The Assassin.

He arrived quickly and with great eagerness. It was hard to tell if The Assassin's business was in a bit of a slump and he was just thankful for the work, or if he simply loved his job. I explained that I not only wanted to engage his services, but I also wanted to learn everything about the business. I was ready to kill.

He grabbed his weapons and ammunition from the back of his truck while I evacuated my wife and kids to the local movie theater. The Assassin and I headed into the shadowed recesses of the garden to take stock of my nemeses. He passed me one of the firearms, and for the first time in my life I held a gun in my hands. It was lighter than I expected. The faux wood grain plastic stock was hollow, cracked, and had been repaired by a well-placed Hot Wheels sticker. The black, cold steel of the barrel was narrow and dented. The trigger light and flimsy, it wiggled loosely from side to side. I knew I was a grown man holding a toy, but I was consoled when I remembered I was taking out a pigeon, not a Russian spy.

The Assassin was thoughtful enough during the weapon assignment process to continually assure me that this was the only way. He too had tried unsuccessfully to humanely remove pigeons from his own home, eventually accepting that the only truly successful method was to very inhumanely blast them out of the sky with a BB gun. Oh, the shock and awe. Guns in hand, we maneuvered our way towards our targets, crouching low, hugging the fence line as we worked our way into position.

Hunting usually takes place in the wild. Wherever you hunt, the one thing that is usually absent is other humans. This is not the case with urban hunting. Especially if the territory you are stalking happens to be on the corner of a busy intersection in a popular neighborhood. Cars are constantly driving by the front and side of the house. A steady parade of people are present—dog walkers, bike riders, and stroller-pushing mothers still giddy from the miracle of birth. Turns out this is a lousy environment if you are sneaking around holding a rifle with the singular intent of taking life. I'm not sure if shooting a pigeon is illegal within Denver city limits, but it sure felt like it was as we crouched behind the shrubbery, hidden from the pigeons and the community.

The problem was one of timing. Our hope was to find a break in the traffic that would allow us to stand up and take a clear shot. That was the easy part. It would become more complicated if we scored a direct hit. Then we'd have to dart out from our cover and, much like golden retrievers, quickly snatch up the carcass and stuff it into a black Hefty leaf bag, then return to the safety of the shrubbery before anybody was aware of the slaughter.

This whole process would take a minute or two. So, waiting for the necessary break in the traffic flow was critical. Nestled to the east of the house between the low hedge and the jungle gym, which had become our make-shift pigeon blind, we quickly realized that with our exposed east and south elevations there would rarely be sufficient gaps to conduct our clandestine operation.

Not confident enough to start a wholesale slaughter in full view of the general public, our only choice was to move our prong of attack to the narrow driveway between my house and the neighbors' property to the west. This fifteen feet of concrete sandwiched between the two bungalows was far more hidden and presented a much better killing field. Cars driving on 32nd Avenue would be traveling too quickly to glance down the driveway. Our only worry was if a neighbor should walk by the end of the drive at the precise moment of the kill. I felt confident we could cross that bridge when we came to it—perhaps by paying them off or, maybe, just rubbing them out.

We repositioned ourselves to the west, pressed up against the fence with a clear view of one of the pigeon's favorite perches. The Assassin had insisted that I take the first shot. It's unwise to argue with an armed assassin, so I agreed. I loaded a pellet into my firearm and pumped the action thirteen times. I stood perfectly still, eyes fixed on the perch as I waited, my body a tightly coiled spring. Senses heightened. Emotions mysteriously absent. Detached from everything except my prey. I had made a choice to kill.

I sensed movement out of the corner of my eye and heard the flutter of wings. A pigeon settled onto its perch facing me, looking me right in the eye. I murmured to him, "Hello, Mr. Pigeon. Meet Mr. Pigeon Killer." I felt nothing. I just had a job to do. I readied my weapon, lined up the plastic sight, my forefinger resting on the wobbly trigger. I exhaled and squeezed. A soft pop sent the bright yellow pellet on its way. It traveled slowly enough to allow me to lower my rifle and watch it arc towards its victim. A hit! Mr. Pigeon toppled off his perch and plummeted to Earth. I grabbed the plastic leaf bag and sprang out to meet the fallen, surprised at how easy and painless the act had been for me. The pigeon hit the ground, cushioned slightly by its own enormous pile of shit. It lay deathly still.

I arrived a second later, body bag in hand. I bent down to remove the evidence. To my surprise, the evidence burst suddenly back to life. One wing flapping madly, the pigeon reared up and leapt skyward in a valiant attempt to escape its murderer. It achieved a height of twenty-four inches before succumbing to gravity and crashing back to the concrete. Again, it launched skyward only to crash back to Earth while spurting and spraying blood over the entire crime scene. With only one wing in full operation, the bird performed his heroic Shakespearean death scene in ever decreasing circles. An astonishing amount of blood was spattered across the driveway. In broad, deep red strokes it flew, as if directed by Quentin Tarantino.

I watched the mêlée with wide eyes, mouth agape, heart racing, stunned at the carnage I had caused with the simple squeeze of a trigger. I had to do something to end this grotesque scene I had started. I grabbed the loaded gun from The Assassin, who was also stunned by the pigeon's refusal to go quietly. I walked towards the thrashing pigeon, trying not to focus on the pair of helpless soft brown doe-eyes. I held the gun to its tiny head, shut my eyes, and once again pulled the trigger. Missed! How the hell could I miss a mostly dead pigeon lying on the ground at point-blank range? But there he was, still twitching, jumping, and spurting.

One of the great benefits of semi-automatic weapons is that when you cock up the first shot, you can quickly and easily rectify the situation with one, two, or even eighteen additional shots in rapid succession. Not so with an air gun. I feebly fumbled for a pellet and loaded it into the chamber, then feverishly pumped one, two, three, *come on!* four, five, six. I felt sympathy for the early musket men—seven, eight, nine—*oh, please ... this is ridiculous ... at this rate the pigeon will have bled out before I can mercifully shoot him again.* Ten, eleven, twelve, thirteen—at last! I took careful aim, kept my eyes open, and ended the despicable task I had started.

The Assassin and I stood in silence and surveyed the scene. A desolate, cold concrete alley. A limp, lifeless carcass. An ever-growing pool of rich, dark blood flowing from its head. Surrounding the corpse was evidence of the deadly struggle. Feathers and blood splattered in a pattern distinct in its depiction of brutality and violence.

I disposed of the body. The Assassin excused himself and returned to his day job, his appetite for death greatly diminished. I was left alone to clean up. I brought out a bucket of soapy water along with some paper towels and mopped up the blood the best I could. It was then that the remorse hit. My curiously absent emotions came back with a vengeance, surging through my body, exaggerated by the task at hand. I thought about the senselessness of what I had done. And how impossible it was to reverse. Any chance I'd had to make it right vanished in a split second as I pulled the trigger.

The remorse is still with me to this day, along with the cooing, the piles of poop, and the pigeons who continue to make my home theirs.

26
JUST A MINUTE

I LOOKED AT MY MOTHER lying serenely in a hospital bed. She did not look like a lady with a little more than a week to live. I had travelled from my home in America to visit and was acutely aware that this would be the last time I spent with my mother alive, but to me she didn't appear to be on her deathbed.

We talked, we laughed and smiled, then she slept while I watched. I knew the cancer was racing unchecked through her frail body and that it was only a matter of time before she would inevitably succumb. My blind naiveté made it easier for me to assume there were months left rather than days.

During my weeklong visit, only once did I realize Sylvia's time was near. One labored breath was all it took. It shattered the pattern of shallow but even breaths I had become accustomed to hearing all week long. This one breath, taken while sleeping, brought the truth flooding back to me. The sheer effort it took to fill her lungs with air, to sustain life for just another moment, shocked me to my core. The shallow even breaths returned, but the stark realization that my mother was teetering on the brink of death haunted me. I moved closer and watched over her as she continued to sleep, fulfilling my duty as a representative of the living, campaigning for life.

A simple bedside lamp cast a dim light throughout the room. Dark shadows waited patiently in the corners. As I gazed upon my mother's face, I allowed my childhood memories to come out to play. I smelled soothing home-cooked meals served on our Formica kitchen table. I saw our smiling faces dappled in muted colors from the Christmas lights on a cheerfully lit tree. I watched my mother struggle as her long slender fingers wrestled with the gear stick of our old, uncooperative yellow Vauxhall Viva. I felt the heat of her body and the bitter resentment of her tears as my ten-year-old arms held her while she sobbed and convulsed uncontrollably after my father had left us. I walked again with her across soft, wet farmland—our heads filled with the salty smells of the Chichester Channel, the brisk breeze attacking our thick woolen jackets, her silver hair dancing in the wind, a spotted dog never far from our heels.

These images and more pulsated through my consciousness, their tempo driven by the rhythmic beat of my heart. I longed to touch and explore every precious moment of our lives together. Knowing these memories would live on brought me peace and eased my sadness.

I could not escape the present for very long, though, however hard I tried. I soon found myself drawn back by the slow metronomic tick of the clock mounted on the wall opposite my mother's hospital bed. I looked up at it—it was so plain. A round, white face ten inches in diameter. Bold, black numbers, and sixty stark black marks around the edge. Two black hands, one long, one short. A thin red second hand that jerkily jumped towards its next rendezvous accompanied by the rhythmic sound of another second passing away.

The unrelenting passage of time. Ever constant. Unyielding. I have often quipped the familiar axioms, "Live every second," "Celebrate the moment," and "Don't let time pass you by," but I never grasped their profundity until that moment. I listened to the seconds tick quietly away.

One after another.

Lost forever.

Gone.

Every tick took my mother closer to her death. But it was only her proximity to death that exaggerated this cruel certainty. I proceed towards my own death at exactly the same pace, just on a different schedule. As I sat there with my mother in the faint light, both of us aging simultaneously, a comforting thought swept through my mind: *I have absolutely no control.*

I took a deep breath and relaxed. Time continued to tick by, second after second after second.

The seconds stopped for my mother at 11:15 a.m. on September the 23rd, 2004, marking the end of her pres-

ence on earth. I often wonder what my mother experienced in that sixteenth minute of that eleventh hour. I
hope that the time constraints there are a little less strin-
gent than here.

27
GOAT LIPS PART II

IT IS CUSTOMARY IN ENGLAND to give your house a name. The origin of certain house names is easy to ascertain. For example, Primrose Cottage, Little Orchard, and The Manor each conjure a certain beginning. Then there are house names that no amount of logical reasoning can decipher. The name of my house in America falls firmly into the latter category.

It was a crystal clear but chilly Colorado morning as I walked across the parking lot of LSI Studios at 5:45 a.m., heading towards the door of Sound Stage Number One to shoot my first ever national commercial. Once inside, I was immediately engulfed by the usual hustle and bustle associated with any filming endeavor. Dozens of people crisscrossed the studio in pairs, talking intensely over clipboards, their footfalls on the concrete floor dampened by foamy sound baffles that hung from the high-beamed ceiling above.

Picking my way carefully over several fat power cables, which snaked their way across the floor, I found the table where I needed to check in. A young lady wearing extremely fashionable eyeglasses (quite possibly for no other reason than fashion) asked for my name.

She scanned her laptop screen and then said knowingly, "Ah, yes, Mr. Taylor. You are—" I felt compelled to finish her sentence. "The lips of the goat," I said quickly. For some reason it was okay for me to say I was the lips of the goat, but it felt odd for other people to tell me I was. She directed me towards makeup, and on the way I paid Craft Services a visit.

Craft Services is where you get fed or, more importantly at this hour of the morning, where I could get coffee. (Why it is called Craft Services I am not at all sure. But Craft Services is what it's called, and if I don't call it Craft Services people will think I don't belong.) With more than my fair share of caffeine, I headed into makeup.

Makeup artists are some of the most chatty and pleasant people on earth. Patti Dallas didn't disappoint. She greeted me with the sort of pep that is rarely seen at six o'clock in the morning. "Ah, yes, Mr. Taylor, you are—" "The lips of the goat," I helpfully interrupted. Moments later I found myself seated in a barber chair, looking directly into a huge mirror with those "I'm a star" light bulbs all around the edges.

Patti was extremely excited to share with me that we were going to be using real goat hair. I didn't have the heart to tell her that I would have been perfectly satisfied with synthetic, but true to her word, out came gobs and gobs of real goat hair, which over the course of the next two hours found its way around my lips and dangled down my chinny, chin, chin.

While I was in makeup, the director paid me a quick visit. He explained that I had to look at the camera and say, "Life is good." He lingered for a while and appeared to be thinking, "There must be more to this than just that." But once he realized there wasn't, he gave a small shrug, as if to say, "Sorry, that's all I have for you." He was saved from this slightly awkward encounter by the ring of his cell phone. He answered it with a fluid motion and was gone—never to be seen by me again.

Once all the coarse and ever-so-slightly goat-smelling hair had been attached to my face, I felt primed and truly ready for some serious goat lip action. A few minutes later, I was summoned to Sound Stage Number One. A small entourage had been sent to collect and deliver me to the set. They all called me Mr. Taylor lots of times, fetched me bottled water, offered me coffee, and generally fussed about me.

I guess their pampering was an attempt to prevent me from throwing a huge hissy-fit and storming off to my trailer (which they had not provided). I decided today was not a tantrum day. I would behave and try not to look too surprised at how much attention I was receiving. I could not help but think, "If this is how they treat the lips of a goat in a beer commercial, what in heaven's name do they do for a real movie star?"

When I entered the set, a bearded man glanced towards me. He was dressed in jeans, a wintry plaid shirt, a well-worn baseball cap, and a tool belt with a large roll of gaffer's tape dangling from it. He quickly turned to his fellow workers and yelled in a deep booming voice, "Talent on the set," at which point they parted like the Red Sea, allowing me access to my chair, which was parked slap-bang in the middle of all the action. Given the circumstances, being described as "talent" was, in my estimation, a bit over the top. Although, I have to confess, all the pandering up to that point had started to affect me.

I briefly considered that it might be necessary for me to climb up onto the chair, gather everybody around me, and explain to them that although I had reached the dizzying heights of goat-lip stardom, it was okay because I could still relate to the little people.

A moment later a young artsy-looking gentleman appeared in front of me and, while half-standing and half-kneeling, he looked straight into my lips, never actually looking me in the eye, and said in a thoughtful tone, "Ah, yes, Mr. Taylor...the lips of the goat." *Dammit! I hate it when I miss my cue.*

Patti the makeup artist stood next to him, armed with a long, thin, pointy pair of scissors. The artsy guy, who turned out to be the assistant director, kept looking directly at my lips and then quickly away and down to my left, then back up to me again. I had no idea why he was doing that. I thought maybe he was simulating an artis-

tic camera movement, but then he repeatedly signaled to
Patti, who leapt forward and snipped at me wildly for a
second. As this continued, I struggled to maintain my lip-
to-eye contact with him. I felt compelled to glance down
to my left. It was just a quick glance, but that was all it
took.

It's hard to mistake a real live goat, especially when
it's parked two feet from you. So here was the real star,
sitting patiently in all his goatliness while I was being
modeled to his likeness. I just sat there thinking, "This
doesn't happen to me every day." Eventually, the snip-
ping stopped and the goat and I were one.

The general activity around me increased as the
goat was removed. I noticed that no one called him Mr.
Goat—they called him Karl. *How did he get on a first-name
basis with everyone?* Out of the chaos, a gentleman slowly
walked towards me, casually holding a blue neoprene
hood in his right hand and looking ominously like an
executioner. He was wearing one of those overly warm
smiles, the kind that dentists assume moments before
saying, "This won't hurt." (Which loosely translates to,
"This will be bloody uncomfortable.")

He proceeded to explain to me that in order to super-
impose my lips onto the goat's face, everything but my
lips would have to be covered. I nodded and a moment
later I was thrust into darkness. The hood was stretched
tightly over my face and secured. I could hear, but everything was muffled and distorted. I felt isolated, similar to
standing in the middle of a large party, but knowing full
well I was the only person not invited.

Suddenly there was a voice in my ear. I recognized it as the Executioner. It was soft and soothing—mainly because the words it was delivering were not. "In order to help you remain still, we're going to clamp your head."

I mumbled some kind of protest, but while mumbling I sensed several bodies moving into close proximity and then the unmistakable feeling of metal touching my skull. I imagined several short rounded men, all with grotesquely warty faces and deformed lumpy backs, dancing around, rubbing their hands in glee while chanting, "Let the clamping begin! Let the clamping begin!"

The clamping was more of an unusual experience than a painful one. To have one's body forced to remain still only highlights the fact that our bodies tend to be in a constant state of motion. As I sat there, clamped, hooded, and waiting, I considered the virtues of not being claustrophobic. I was jerked out of this thought by a new voice—which was a good thing, because I was being forced against my will to consider experimenting with a slight case of claustrophobia. I listened intently through the spandex to this new voice that sounded remarkably like my own.

The English accent said in a polite tone, "Hello, Mr. Taylor, I'm your voice coach." At this point I thought, _You have got to be kidding. A voice coach!? I only have three words. And they are not very long words. To be exact, ten letters in total. Life. Is. Good._

And anyway, why didn't you come and visit me during the two hours of makeup instead of waiting for me to be clamped, deafened, and blinded? And besides, if you're already here, why *don't you just do it yourself?* But then I remembered. *Ah — I have very special lips.*

The English voice said, "Mr. Taylor, this is how I want you to say it." Then he said, "Life is good."

I said, "Life is good."

He said, "Good." Then he repeated it. "Life is good."

I repeated it.

He repeated it.

I repeated it.

He said, "Good." And that was that. I wondered how much he charged per letter.

Once the extensive voice coaching was over, another voice spoke into my ear. This one I recognized as the director. He said, "Mr. Taylor, just face the camera (as if my severely clamped head was going to face anywhere else) and after a few seconds, say 'Life is good.'"

I heard a muffled "Action," and that is exactly what I did — ten or fifteen times. I heard a muffled, "Cut, I think we've got it." Instantly, there were several hands upon me, the clamp was released, the hood pulled up and off, revealing a hot, sweaty, and blinking me. There were a few "Thank you, Mr. Taylors," and I was free to go.

As I left the set, the entire crew applauded, which I thought was a very nice touch. My lip work must have moved them. Patti quickly removed all extraneous hair, my voucher was signed, and I found myself wandering across the LSI parking lot, returning to the car I had parked three hours earlier.

The commercial aired during the first Monday Night Football game of the season and continued to play for six weeks. I never got to see it due to the fact that I don't watch a lot of TV and I'm way too disorganized to actually ask the producer for a copy. And besides, if I couldn't watch it with Karl, what would be the point?

One morning, I was at home and heard the mailman. I sauntered over to the mailbox and collected the letters. I thumbed through them and stopped at the one from Donna Baldwin Talent. I opened it and smiled—for two reasons.

First, the check was for a substantial amount of money. Second, in the area reserved for "description of job" was clearly printed "Goat Lips." The residual checks kept coming and I kept smiling. When, eventually, no more checks appeared, my wife and I made an appointment with a mortgage broker and the down payment and expenses for our first house were covered almost exactly to the penny.

That August, my wife Susan and I happily moved into Goat Lip Cottage, where, I must say, life is good.

In Gratitude

COLLABORATION IS AT THE HEART of my creative process. I am nothing without the constant support, love, and wisdom of the people who surround me. This project has been no different.

Thanks to the many people who have attended my readings, especially Vince Taliercio and Rob Orosz.

Thanks to my wonderful wife Susan who has always allowed me to be me, and to my amazing kids, Maitland and Alastair. The three of you make every day an adventure and life a joy to live.

Thanks to my longtime A.C.E. Entertainment business partners, Linda Klein and Barbara Gehring, for endless hours of laughter while we explore the art of comedy.

Thanks to Paul Orosz for his continual support, vast depth of knowledge, and appreciation of well-made drinks.

Thanks to my publisher and editor, Donna Mazzitelli of Merry Dissonance Press, for making the tales flow and for gracefully pulling all the pieces together.

Thanks to my illustrator, Catherine McNeil, whose pen, ink, and creative flair added so much. I had no idea that wine and cheese were such a strong creative catalyst.

Thanks to my editor and dear friend, Bobby Haas, whose insightful comments scribbled in the margins pushed me to do better and greatly shaped my voice. You rock.

Lastly, a huge thank you to the immensely gifted Linda Klein. Your patience and belief in me is humbling, your genius inspiring, and your laughter contagious. This book is as much yours as mine.

About the Author

MATTHEW TAYLOR was transplanted to Colorado from the small sailing village of Itchenor, England. He has been a professional actor, improviser, storyteller, and humorist for the last twenty-five years, working throughout the United States and internationally. He is a partner of A.C.E. Entertainment, which over the last fourteen years has written and produced over fifty original shows, and is currently touring their smash hit, *Girls Only – The Secret Comedy of Women.* Encouraged from the popularity of the A.C.E. show, *Tales of an Englishman,* Matthew continued to commit his stories to paper, which have now been compiled into the book, *Goat Lips: Tales of a Lapsed Englishman.*

Matthew has a long history of coaching theatre, storytelling, and the art of improvisation. He formed *Persuasion through Narrative* in 2010 to teach communication skills through the use of narrative and has quickly gained a strong reputation, especially within the legal profession and educational institutions.

Matthew loves to bike, ski, sail, and is proud to be a husband and a father of two fabulous children (who continually keep him on his toes and laughing constantly).

Let's Stay Connected

To stay connected, please be sure to find me online by visiting my website at www.matthewtaylor.com. Or connect with me on Facebook, LinkedIn, Twitter and YouTube. You can also contact me via email at matthew@matthewtaylor.com. I would love to hear from you.

And one last favor …

If you have enjoyed this book, please be sure to visit my Amazon book page and leave a review.

Thank you!

About the Press

Merry Dissonance Press is a book producer/indie publisher of works of transformation, inspiration, exploration, and illumination. MDP takes a holistic approach to bringing books into the world that make a little noise and create dissonance within the whole in order that ALL can be resolved to produce beautiful harmonies.

Merry Dissonance Press works with its authors every step of the way to craft the finest books and help promote them. Dedicated to publishing award-winning books, we strive to support talented writers and assist them to discover, claim, and refine their own distinct voice. **Merry Dissonance Press** is the place where collaboration and facilitation of our shared human experiences join together to make a difference in our world.

For more information, visit http://merrydissonancepress.com/.

MAR 2 2 2016

CPSIA information can be obtained at www.ICGtesting.com
Printed in the USA
LVOW11s0205070116

469485LV00007B/856/P

9 781939 919021